ONE MOTHER

OF A

PORN

STAR

BOOK ONE OF FOUR

A TRUE LIFE SAGA OF ABUSE, VIOLENCE,
AND
ONE WOMAN'S STRUGGLE TO PROTECT
THE CHILDREN SHE LOVES

NANCY TURNER

First Edition/Book One of Four/2013
e-Book Publishing/Paperback

Cover Design by Derek Murphy

All Images Copyright © 2013 by Nancy Turner aka
All rights reserved - Library of Congress

ISBN: 978-0692459935

ACKNOWLEDGMENTS

Dedicated To:

My Brother
Without him, I would not be here today.

To my Amazing Son
For being the light of my life and sharing your story with me.

To my Psychotherapist, Betty T.
You brought me through that Dark Forest.
I will forever be grateful to you.

To God
For sending Angels to guide and protect me.
Especially, the "Whispering Angel."

TABLE OF CONTENTS

1

≈

Why Me Lord

The year was 1951. My third grade teacher, Mrs. Anderson, asked each student to write a short biography the first day of school.

I wrote the following short essay:

I'm Debbie Henderson, a naïve, feisty eight-year-old, tree-climbing tomboy with sky blue hypnotic eyes. My straight blonde hair resembles windblown wheat. In the summertime, my olive skin tans like an Indian. My small town Southern family is dirt poor. I have five dresses to my name, but I prefer blue jeans. We live in a small shotgun house. My oval face has a roundish nose with a chicken-pox scar. I love my dog and horse. I can be a bit sensitive due to my hard childhood. Frequently, I play in the Dummy Line with friends. I believe I once lived as a young Indian male with a strong fighting spirit, and I could run like the wind.

An elderly neighbor named Richard Farmer invited me to watch him carve and paint a fishing lure two weeks ago. After he finished, he smiled at me. "Are you ready for some of Rena's best chocolate cake?"

I nodded and followed him into their kitchen. He uncovered the cake and cut me a big slice. Then he turned away from me with a funny grin. I had a mouth full of moist cake, as he slowly faced me. *"Would you like to come here and hold this?"*

When I peered at his hands my eyes froze like giant ice cubes. I couldn't breathe. One of his hands motioned for me to come closer. The table between us was my only hope of escape.

"Come on, honey, just touch it. It's soft and smooth."

"Stay away from me, or I'll tell my mom!"

✳ ✳ ✳

Many years passed by. I dashed through the LAX terminal toward my flight gate. I took a detour into a newsstand and happily purchased my first book to read on my long Paris flight. I noticed several people were waiting to purchase the same book with a unique cover. *Bingo!* I bought the last copy. It must be my lucky day. I paid the clerk and hustled toward my flight gate. I was the last one to board, so I hurried to my seat, buckled up and held the book for takeoff.

Later, a striking stewardess named Janice served me a Diet Coke. I focused on the book title, *One Mother of a Porn Star.*

As I glanced out the small window beside me I saw a shooting star. Hopefully, it is a positive omen. The cover enticed me to turn to the first page to read an unusual journey.

✳ ✳ ✳

My name is Debbie Austin. I'm a divorced mom with two children. I have a daughter and a son born five years apart.

Crystal's long blonde curls, green eyes and model nose gave her an exceptional look growing up. She was smart, but she had her dad's bad horrible temper by the age of two.

Stacy took after his dad, Tim Malone. He has dark brown hair and eyes. His eyes were rich with mischief, even as a baby. He proved to be highly intelligent and good looking.

Honestly, I never dreamed someone in my family would ever become a famous porn star. *I'm sure I'm not alone.*

Mother raised me in a super strict Church of Christ home from the time I was born.

Even so, I married too many times and so did she. My children had different fathers. I raised them the best I knew how. God came first, family second and "Do unto others" third. The church never believed in dancing, drinking, swearing, wearing shorts, fornication, or anything that even smacked of porn. They had well over a hundred other super strict rules like no musical instruments. It was odd that they allowed speakers and microphones. That always seemed like a contradiction to me.

Momma was Claudine Henderson to her friends. She was short, stocky, attractive, wore glasses, and she loved to gossip on the telephone. She took me to church every time the doors opened.

When I was seven she married her third husband. His name was Harry Henderson. He never struck me as friendly because it was rare to see him smile. He looked and sounded more like a grumpy country farmer. He had an Assembly of God background and ran a Mobile gas station. Their small wedding was held in Granny's living room. I was their flower girl. Come honeymoon time I surprised everyone. "I want to go, too."

I cried as I realized they were leaving me behind, so Harry gave me a shiny silver dollar. It didn't help. I remained inconsolable. He made me a promise. "When we return, I'll get you a big surprise." I watched them drive away and cried. It felt like Mother had just abandoned me for this cold stranger.

A month passed by. Harry actually surprised me with a small black Cocker Spaniel puppy. He named him Smokey Joe. It thrilled me until they cut off his little tail. I cried, but in no time he and I became inseparable playmates.

One day, Momma sat me down in our small kitchen. "Harry plans to adopt you and change your name to Debbie Henderson."

I shrugged. "I guess." Smokey and I ran outside to play.

✳ ✳ ✳

Harry and I got along for a time, until they began taking me to the VFW twice a week. Mother would practice with the ladies' drill team. Harry hung out in the bar area to play poker and get drunk. The place totally bored me, until one day I saw a row of slot machines near a back wall. I figured out that Harry would give me a handful of nickels once he was drunk. I'd play the slots when no one was looking, since I was under age.

It was difficult to understand why we lived in two different worlds. Twice on Sundays and once on Wednesday nights, we went to church. That made the VFW feel dishonest.

Sometimes Momma drove me to the VFW and parked. "Go inside and convince Harry to leave before he spends all our money."

"Why would he listen to me?"

"He's like a love-sick puppy around you when he drinks."

Funny thing is Momma was right. When I approached him at a poker table, I would get his attention. "Time to go home."

He'd gush. "Anything for my sweet little gal."

Two Sundays later, Mother met Rena Farmer at church. She was a sweet older lady with polio paralyzed legs. She needed a walker to get around. Her husband, Richard, was a retired rugged-looking fisherman with a gray mustache and thinning hair. He wore Khaki clothes and drove a beat-up truck with a camper.

✳ ✳ ✳

Weeks later Momma took my hand. "Our neighbors, Rena and Richard, want us to come over today for a visit." It became a weekly trip to visit Rena. She enjoyed baking us fresh cakes or cookies. Richard had a workshop on their back porch where he made fishing lures. He rarely said much. During one visit, I decided to go outside and play with Smokey Joe. Richard followed me outside. "Come over anytime. I'll show you how I make fishing lures."

"I guess so." I shrugged and took off running with Smokey Joe on my heels. We raced to the Dummy Line. I liked to go there to fish for crawdads. Sometimes, I'd attempt to walk across the long black sewer pipe with a small stream below it.

In a week, Momma drove Rena to a grocery store. I decided to go watch Richard make a new lure. In no time, he carved and painted a long lure and hung it up to dry. "Are you ready for some of Rena's best chocolate cake?"

"Sure." I nodded and followed him into the kitchen.

He uncovered the cake and cut me a slice. I watched him turn away as I took a big bite of cake. He slowly turned back around with an odd grin. "Want to come here and hold this?"

My blue eyes froze. His pants were unzipped. I could see his wrinkled penis staring at me from his hand. I'd never seen one before. I held my breath in shock. He motioned for me to come closer. I choked. I knew my only hope of escape was to trick him. I moved right; he moved right. I charged left; he blocked me. Only the round table protected me from his grasp.

"Come on, honey, it won't hurt you. It's smooth and soft."

"Get away from me!"

"I want you to touch it, so I'll feel better."

"You're crazy!"

I knew I had to make a run for the backdoor to escape. My feet took off toward that door. As I whipped past him, he grabbed my long hair. I screamed in pain. "Let go of me, or I'll tell Momma what you did."

He pulled me toward his penis. I bit his hand with a vengeance. "You're a dirty old man!" Then, I ran for the back door where Smokey Joe had waited for me.

I never told anyone about that incident. I knew it would crush Rena if Richard went to jail. I worried that it might destroy her, so I decided to steer clear of him after that day.

✳ ✳ ✳

That weekend Momma drove me to the VFW. I can still recall that drunken laughter and smell of thick cigarette smoke. My long blonde braids swished, as I eased toward my barstool perch. It was a wobbly stool at a small bar in the back of the club. I spotted Harry across the room. He was still wearing his Magnolia service station uniform, playing poker for money and chain-smoking. That evening he looked drunker than usual, so I veered around him and ran smack into someone else.

"If it isn't my sweet little Debbie come to see me again."

Dear God, what is Richard doing here?

I noticed he had a bandage over my bite mark on his hand. *Most likely, he fears uncomfortable questions.* I hurriedly made a fast U-turn away from his outstretched hands. In seconds, I was safely atop my special barstool.

The muscular bartender didn't mind me watching him mix drinks or open beer cans. Hours later, my intrigue about the taste of beer grew insatiable. A huge brainstorm hit me. *When the bartender looks away, I'm gonna snatch an empty beer can from the bar and get a little taste of that stuff.*

My wish seemed his command. He turned his back. In a flash, I grabbed a can and swigged the remaining bitter contents in a hurried gulp. *Not bad. Each time he turns away I'll secret another can from the bar counter and finish it off and then another and another.*

Things went fine for a few glorious moments until a strange sickness clutched my stomach. The room began to rock-and-sway. I raced for the restroom. A blurry figure of a man stepped into my path with outstretched arms. "Are you looking for me, sugar?"

It was Richard again. I nearly choked on my own vomit. "Go away!" I pushed past him and scurried into the restroom.

Mother followed me. She was still wearing her long lime green, drill team dress and an ugly expression. "You know better than to yell at Richard."

"I'm sick." I threw up almost as if to prove it.

She slapped a wet paper towel on my throbbing forehead and gripped each of my eyelids one-at-a-time with her thumb to inspect each of my bloodshot eyes. "What have you been doing?"

I shrugged innocently and clutched my queasy stomach. As I peered into the smudged mirror, I saw a ghost-like figure with red eyes staring at me. I soon realized it was me.

Momma grabbed my arm. "Go apologize to Richard."

"I can't. I'm too sick."

"Go lay down in my car."

I slowly weaved through the poker tables toward the exit. I could feel Momma's hard stare on my back. Out of nowhere came a familiar tattooed arm. It blocked my way. It was Harry. He oozed one of his slurred adulations. "Where's my little gal going?"

"I'm sick. I just threw up. I going to Momma's car."

He pulled me close to his chest and squeezed my waist. My stomach revolted in flip-flops.

"I have to go, Harry." He grinned at me like a lovesick bleary-eyed puppy.

"Guys, this here's my good luck charm. She's my little Debbie gal." Three grungy poker players nodded, continued to puff their smelly cigarettes and study their cards. Harry's breath was a sickening combination of smoke and beer. That awful smell reawakened my Montezuma's Revenge, and Richard was walking toward me again. I frantically struggled to pull free from Harry's grip.

"Okay, honey-doll, I'll make you feel better if you go look in my truck. There's a big surprise in the glove box for you."

My eyes failed to focus. My ears kept ringing. He leaned close to kiss me on the lips. I turned my head just in time to avoid his beer-drenched mouth from touching mine. *To this day, I still get nauseous from the smell of beer.*

Once inside his truck, I found a photo of a chestnut brown horse and a sales receipt with the name *Dolly* scribbled on it. Harry wouldn't do that for me, would he? *I don't believe it.*

Days later, Harry brought Dolly home. The moment I saw her big brown eyes, I fell in love. I raced my bicycle a mile home from school to ride Dolly. She even allowed me to put Smokey Joe on her back for an occasional ride.

✵ ✵ ✵

Several years passed and summer arrived. It was time for me to go to Bluebird Camp for two weeks. Smokey Joe followed me, as I ran to Dolly and hugged her. "Goodbye. I'll miss you while I'm gone." Smokey gave my cheek a big wet kiss before I left.

When I returned home, Dolly's pen was empty. My heart sank. I raced home and found Harry. "Where's Dolly?"

"I sold her and bought you a better horse."

"There is no better horse! I want Dolly back."

"Sure there is, just you wait and see."

Tears welled up in my eyes. I cornered Mother in our small kitchen. "Why did Harry sell Dolly?"

"He was drunk and lost her in a poker game, but he plans to buy you another horse." I scurried to my room, shut the door and cried myself to sleep. Losing Dolly devastated me beyond words. I avoided that old drunk for weeks.

Debbie and her Beloved "Dolly"

✳ ✳ ✳

A month later, Harry drove up in his truck and came inside our back porch. "Debbie, your new horse is over in his pen. Try to make friends with him and feed him some sugar cubes. In no time, you can ride him without a saddle or a bridle. That's how the kids who owned him did it." I grabbed the sugar cubes from his open hand and raced out the backdoor in total excitement.

I spent a whole week grooming, feeding and making friends with my new black horse. I finally decided it was time to go for a ride. I climbed onto the tall wooden gate, fed him some sugar cubes and slid onto his back. He froze and then took off down the field faster than a bolt of lightning. That horse bucked me for all he was worth, as I clutched his mane for dear life and endured what seemed like a thirty minute wild bronco ride. In truth, it took no more than thirty seconds. That crazy horse raced straight toward the back fence bucking and kicking all the way. I flew through the air and landed in a blueberry bush full of stickers. It was surrounded by sand and gravel. The blow knocked the breath out of me. I was hurt and scared at the same time, until my breath finally returned.

After I managed to stand up, I realized I was a bloody mess. It hurt to walk home. I saw Harry's truck pull into our driveway. I glared at him. "You can sell that stupid horse. He's no dang good." Then, I trooped inside to doctor my numerous wounds.

My experience taught me two hard lessons that day. Never believe everything an alcoholic says and always refer to lesson number one when in doubt.

✳ ✳ ✳

As summer ended, Mother soon learned the same hard lesson. Frantic screams awakened me one night. Harry was drunk and had hit her several times. I remember hearing her cry. Harry made a slurred apology. "I'll never do it again, honey, honest!"

After more severe episodes, Momma finally called our small-town Sheriff Woody Sheen. "I need your help. Harry's drunk again. This is the third time he's hit me. It has to stop."

Harry was close friends with Sheriff Woody, so he was allowed him to sleep it off in jail overnight. Woody drove Harry home the following day and let him out at the curb.

It didn't surprise me when Harry's drinking and violence escalated. That proved to be the last straw. Momma had him committed to the State Hospital to dry out. They gave him pills that made him sick if he took another drink. When he came home, I saw him flush his pills down the toilet. Within in weeks, he resumed drinking and smoking but something new showed up called *blackouts*. The best news was that he never hit Momma again. Bad news quickly showed up, too. He managed to get drunk and spoil almost every special occasion we had for many years to come.

✳ ✳ ✳

During my junior high years, I made friends with a homely girl with enormous boobs. All the other kids called her *Wild Child Wanda*. She easily convinced me to slip out of our house and go see a midnight movie or a drive-in movie with her and some guys on Saturday nights. I cleverly oiled several door hinges and hoped that my exit would go unnoticed.

Momma never said a word about it, yet I'm sure she knew every time I left. *Her lack of discipline made me feel unloved and invisible.* Plus, it was rare for her to ever touch or hug me. The only times I can recall getting an occasional hug was when she told me, "Goodnight," after I went to bed. She never voluntarily uttered the words, "I love you," my whole childhood.

It was many years later, and after two of years of intense psychotherapy to deal with Momma's lack of love and other major issues, that I tried to change things. I finished one of our phone conversations differently. "I love you, Momma." The phone line went silent. She hung up. I had wanted so much for her to say, "I love you," back to me.

I did the same thing with my older half-brother, Matt Curtis. He was extremely attractive and smoked like a fiend. His nose had an unusual shape. It was flat on the end. He also had warm blue eyes, and he served in the Air Force during the Korean War. There was a cold stern, authoritarian side to him. He was married, and they had four children. Their first child, Candy, died of leukemia when she turned two.

The first time I ended my call to Matt with, "I love you," I sensed that my words had touched his heart. I practically felt his tears through the telephone, but it took him much longer to finally respond with, "I love you, Sis."

When Momma died six years later, Matt called me afterward to visit. He told me about a phone call he had from her, when I was in the seventh grade. "I may have to put Debbie into a girl's school. She's hanging out with a wild girl named Wanda. I just can't keep her in line."

Keep me in line? That's a laugh. When did Mother ever try to keep me in line or control me?

"If she had tried it, Matt, I would have run away."

"I know you would have. I ran away from your dad, Coot, and joined the Air Force. That's how I ended up in the Korean War. Honey, your dad was a cruel hateful man. I hated to leave you behind with him, and I had to escape from his hell."

✳ ✳ ✳

Our discussion triggered my worst memory of my Dad's cruelty. I was only four-years-old. My three little kittens were dirty, so I decided to bathe them. Mother finally hung up the phone, scolded me and made me sit in Daddy's rocking chair. "Just wait until I tell your daddy what you did today."

"My kitties were dirty," I whimpered. I had already suffered because of Daddy's bad temper. She forced me to sit there for hours and wait on him to return from work for my punishment.

He eventually flung the back screen door open. I could hear her tattle on me. "Debbie bathed those little kittens. They might catch a cold and die."

I shuddered at the sound of Daddy's black belt, as it ripped through his belt loops and shook the air. He charged into the living room toward me like a raging bull and snapped his belt to make it crack. I half expected him to slice me into small pieces any second.

Imagine a four-year-old watching this scene. It had to look like a horror movie. His belt hit my left arm. I screamed in pain and stood up in the rocker. He kicked it over backwards. I flew through the air, landed on my head and began to cry.

He gripped my arm, drug me out our front door and down the steep steps onto the hot sidewalk. The next thing I knew, I was dangling in mid-air by one of my arms. He proceeded to beat me with his belt, while I screamed bloody murder. "Momma, help me!" My momma never came. The searing pain was unbearable. *Is he going to beat me until I die?*

When the beating finally ended, he forced me to sit on the hot cement steps by the sidewalk. "Stay put until you quit bawling."

Huge red whelps rapidly rose on my throbbing legs and body. I cried for the longest time. A few people walked past me on the sidewalk, but no one stopped to comfort me. Momma was still nowhere in sight. *No one in this world loves me. No one! Why didn't Mother come outside to help me?*

✷ ✷ ✷

That cruel beating must have launched my serious stubborn streak. Harry's hatefulness only made it ten times worse. By the time I entered the ninth grade, he began to cough up blood. He would pass out for longer and longer periods of time. He finally went to see

Doctor Howard. "Harry, either stop drinking and smoking or you'll be dead in one year."

We were relieved when Harry gave up both of his bad habits. Unfortunately, he grew even more belligerent and overbearing with me after he dried out. I became his *Number One Enemy*.

Our arguments grew more intense every day. Often, he would march into the living room while I was watching TV, and he'd change the channel. Heated words always followed. "You and Momma have another TV in your bedroom."

During my freshman year, I signed up for the band and became Head Majorette. That meant I would be wearing short costumes in parades, pep rallies, and football games. The Church of Christ ladies immediately labeled me a sinner and an outcast. Their whispers were vicious, until Granny caught wind of them. She voiced her extreme displeasure to someone. "I donated the land this church sits on years ago. Now, I want the gossip about Debbie to cease." *Funny how those icy stares quickly melted.*

It was no wonder I began to look to boys for the love and attention I craved from Momma. I dreamed of the day I'd get married, have a baby and move far away from *Horrible Harry*. In his eyes, I could do no right.

Many nights, I sat on our front porch steps and cried desperate lonely tears for hours. Smokey Joe would show up to nuzzle my arm or lick my hand and comfort me. He couldn't say it, but his big brown eyes spoke volumes. He loved me as no one else in the world ever did. Those were some of the saddest years of my life.

One day, I learned from Mother that Smokey Joe had visited every female dog in town, especially when they were in heat. "How did you find that out, Momma?"

"The City Dog Catcher told me."

I laughed my sides off. "My Smokey is quite a Casanova."

✳ ✳ ✳

During my sophomore year in high school, I met Cody Barnes. He was a tall lanky senior at school who drove a fire engine red Studebaker. He gave me a young Siamese kitten. I named her Pyewacket after the cat in the Kim Novak movie, *Bell, Book and Candle*. In short order, I received Cody's class ring and wore it around my neck that showed others we were going steady.

Easter morning arrived. His parents went out of town. We slept together for the first time in his bedroom. He drove me home at four a.m. and kissed me on our front porch. I slipped through the doorway and got a big jolt.

Momma was sitting in her chair in her nightgown. A large Bible was draped across her lap. She closed it, stood up without a word and went to bed. It was as if I didn't exist. *Will I ever get free of this family where no one loves me enough to talk to me when I need it? My rising invisibility factor felt even harder to swallow.*

Momma expected me to be dressed for church at ten a.m. later that morning, so I was.

One day in *June, 1960*, Cody cried when I returned his class ring. Roland Powers found out I was available. He had a pug nose and dreamy blue eyes. His hair was cut in a flattop with Elvis sideburns and sweptback ducktails. He brimmed with sex appeal and overconfidence. He loved to play golf and hung out with older guys. He and his best friend, Stacy Carter, had frequent fist fights. Somehow, they remained friends. Roland drove a '55 blue-and-white Chevy. I remember the first time I saw him. I was in grade school. He was in junior high. We were in the Band together a year later, and my schoolgirl crush shifted into high gear.

One of my girlfriends and I decided to drag Main Street one night, after I broke up with Cody my sophomore year. It didn't take Roland long to ask me to be his girl. We rapidly spent many evenings at a nearby lake indulging in heavy petting. We began to frequent the local drive-in theater, and we went too far. Ironically, *A Summer Place*, starring Sandra Dee and Troy Donohue, was on the big screen that year. They were doing the same thing we were.

I'll never forget the summer day he drove me downtown and parked on a side street. "Where are we going, Roland?"

"I want you to see Daddy's new store." He took me by the hand and led me into a small liquor store.

"Why are we going in here?"

"This is now Daddy's liquor store."

"You're kidding me." I knew this spelled big trouble with my family. I dreaded the whispers. *Have you heard that Debbie Henderson's boyfriend's family owns a sinful liquor store?*

We dated my junior and senior year, even though Roland was mostly away at college. Midway through my last year in high school, my life took an unexpected turn. Harry and I had heated words over the TV again. He marched into the living room and changed the channel in the middle of a movie I was watching.

"Why do you always do that? My movie's almost over."

"I bought that TV, so we're going to watch what I want when I want in the living room."

"Can't you wait thirty minutes until my movie is over?"

Without a word, he flopped into his recliner. Momma hurriedly showed up and sat in her rocking chair. *Unbelievable!*

I jumped up, went to my room, played my 45 records, and I pouted on my bed. *I just don't matter to anyone! That familiar thought played in my head like a worn out record all night long.*

When I came in from school, Momma called me into the living room. Harry was standing beside her with a sullen scowl. She began to wring her hands. "Harry just gave me an ultimatum. Either you leave, or he does. What should I do?"

Her question dumbfounded me and flipped my eighteen-year-old reality upside-down. *Why must I choose the future of Mother's marriage? Aren't they the adults here?*

After some deep thought, I announced. "I graduate in six months, so I'll move in with Granny and Pop Sherman." I hurriedly packed my things and moved out within the hour.

Granny proved to be a super strict disciplinarian who tolerated nothing. Finally, there was someone in my life who didn't beat me with a strap belt or make me feel invisible. She loved me enough to say, "No late hours" and "Granny loves you."

Sadly, her strict curfew rapidly caused lots of friction in my relationship with Roland. Two months later, I broke up with him on a snowy afternoon in January while we talked in my car. Strange as it may seem, Mother asked me to move back home. Harry shocked me. He was nice to me for a short time. I often wondered why everyone was so happy that I broke up with Roland.

✳ ✳ ✳

It was thirty years later, when Roland returned into my life and revealed a shocking secret. "Not only did I make back door liquor deliveries to Daddy's customers, many of them were your church members, elders and deacons. Debbie, my best customer was your Pop Sherman." His newsflash almost bowled me over.

I approached Mother and quizzed her. "Granny turned on Roland for an important reason. She caught him making weekly whiskey deliveries to Pop Sherman's back bedroom door, so she set out to break you two up. She couldn't have your boyfriend delivering sinful booze to her husband."

I could only shake my head and ponder. *Granny and Pop Sherman went to church every time the doors were open.* One day we're church folks, and years later I discover that my grandfather secretly ordered two bottles of whiskey every week from Roland's family. Needless to say, I was shocked to discover how hard Granny worked to end my relationship with Roland, thirty years ago. *Can my life be any more dysfunctional?*

✳ ✳ ✳

Within weeks of breaking up with Roland my Senior Year, I met an attractive quiet young man from the Air Force named Jack Harmon. He had a pug nose, great physique, sparkling German blue eyes and short blond hair. He was soft spoken and a bit rigid. He visited our church for several weeks and asked me out. We dated, fell in love and four weeks later, he proposed marriage on Valentine's Day. Jack surprised me with a small diamond ring. Momma seemed unusually happy about our marriage news. I was thrilled that I would graduate in three months. *Finally there is light at the end of my unhappiness tunnel. No more opposing worlds for me.*

On March first, we had an all-class meeting in the gym. To my surprise, Principal Yates announced that I was one of the top twenty graduates in my class. Each of us received an Honors certificate and pin during the presentation.

That night, Jack took me out to dinner to celebrate. I drove us in my pink-and-gray '55 Chevy that Harry gave me when I entered high school. After dinner, I drove home and parked in the driveway beside our house. Jack kissed me. We foolishly made out in the front seat of my car. By mid-April, I realized I was in trouble. Big trouble. I missed my period.

I broke the news to Jack. "We're going to have a baby."

He didn't take it well. "I'm not ready for a kid."

Days later, he took a leave of absence from the Air Force and went home to see his former girlfriend for a week. When he returned and knocked on Mother's front door, I opened it to meet a different Jack. He was now a cold distant stranger that I didn't know.

He snarled. "I want my ring back. I don't want a baby."

"What am I supposed to do?"

"That's your problem."

"We were engaged to be married."

"Not anymore."

Devastation swept through my veins. I was scared to death. Even so, I returned his engagement ring. *I have nowhere to turn. I'm a teenager having a baby with no idea of what to do. I've never even changed a diaper.*

In the sixties, news about any pregnancy at school spread like wildfire in small towns. It didn't take Mother long to realize I was in trouble. "Did you miss your period this month?"

"No." I lied out of fear and shame. Days later, I bought a huge bottle of aspirin, sat in our living room alone and swallowed a big handful of pills. I felt the only way out was to end my life. It was something I'd never considered before.

God had other plans for me that day. I suddenly threw up the pills, went to bed with a terrible headache and slept until noon the next day.

Six days later, Mother approached me. "You still haven't had your period. You have to get married right away!"

"Why? It's only six weeks until I graduate. I want to wait."

"If you don't get married immediately, I'll be the scandal of the church and the whole town. I can't let that happen."

"How can I get married? There's no groom!" I dashed out the door and drove to school in tears.

Mother's selfishness broke my already distraught heart. *Why is her reputation all that matters? Isn't my reputation also important?* Horrible humiliation is about to flood my life, if word gets out.

It was during this painful crisis that I decided to have my long blonde hair cut off. It wasn't clear to me why I did it. Afterward, I stared in the mirror and wept.

Momma must have twisted some arms because a few church members spoke to Jack. "You must do the right thing and marry Debbie. There's a baby to consider."

Three agonizing weeks later, Jack approached me as I left a girlfriend's house. "I guess we need to get married."

"That's the only thing I know to do."

"It seems we're stuck." His reluctance wasn't assuring.

Mother insisted we get our blood tests for our marriage license right away. Jack did fine when they drew his blood. When I stood up afterward, I promptly fainted.

She made arrangements for our wedding at the Air Force Base Chapel and eagerly paid for everything. *May eighth is a day I will always regret. I vaguely recall seeing two of my close girlfriends there. The wedding was a miserable blur.*

My only hope of graduating was if no one noticed our marriage license in the local newspaper. They printed marriage applications every week. I stayed on pins and needles, and I prayed I could at least graduate.

With only nine school days left, I spent most of my class time asking friends to sign my annual. The rest of the time, I was in the restroom throwing up my heels. Pregnancy didn't agree with me. I prayed and prayed. *God, please let me graduate with my class and escape untold humiliation.*

I still remember the day I was sitting in Mrs. Johnson's English Class. A student aid hand-delivered a note for me. "Principal Yates requests you come to his office."

When I sat down, I noticed his brown-rimmed glasses were on the end of his nose. He had been my eighth grade teacher in junior high. I knew that was a bad sign. "I need to ask you some questions. There was a report that you are married."

"Who told you that?"

"I can't say, but you know the rules. Married students can't participate in anything in school like..."

"Mr. Yates, there are only nine school days left."

"I understand that you married recently. Is that correct?"

In that moment, I knew what was coming. I chose to lie rather than suffer the unfair consequences. "No, we got our marriage license, and we're engaged. That's all."

Dear God, I only need nine more days to graduate. Is that too much to ask?

"I'll take your word for now."

I nodded and quickly returned to class to finish out my day. Two days later came a second note from Mr. Yates. His glasses were on his desk. His cheeks were bright red.

"Did you get married on May eighth?"

I hung my head in silence.

"Am I correct?"

I sat there like a motionless zombie. I wanted to vanish forever. I wouldn't answer him.

"The newspaper printed your marriage license last week."

"It's good for thirty days."

"A friend of yours told me you were married at Perkins Air Force Base. Is that right?"

I stared into his strained eyes. "Yes." My heart sank. *Why did a friend blow the whistle on me like that?*

He spewed out the school's list of rules. "If you want your graduation to become official, you must return your Honors pin and certificate; you can't go on the Senior Day outing; you can't perform with the Band at their last performance; you will never see your cap and gown."

I broke into tears and pleaded. "Momma already paid for my cap and gown. Can I at least try them on and have my picture made?"

He practically shouted, "No!"

Word swept through my school faster than a wildfire. Many classmates began to gossip and snicker about me behind my back. So-called friends avoided me in disgust. One former friend made sure I knew that Mr. Yates gave my Honors certificate and pin to the daughter of one of the high school teachers. *It crushed me. Why should she get my Honors recognition?* She didn't make the grades I did to earn it. She has no right to have them.

When I walked in that day, Harry and Mother were waiting in the living room for me. "Pack your things and move right now."

I stared at them in stunned silence. *My world just collapsed around me at school and now this.* "And where am I supposed to go?"

"To live with your husband. The bedroom suite stays here."

"I'll put my things in my car and leave."

She snatched my car keys from the dresser and left.

"You and Harry gave me that car and the bedroom suite. I see you're doing what you taught me not to do. You're being Indian Givers!"

I packed my suitcase, grabbed some clothes and lugged them six blocks to find Jack. He was staying with one of his Air Force buddies and his wife. When I arrived, they said that we could stay with them for a few weeks. Jack vanished three days later. He went home again to be with his former girlfriend. When he returned, our marriage rapidly whirred into a *Nightmare from Hell.* He began to stay out late, get drunk, and he grew more difficult and angry with me over silly stuff. He was like Daddy and Harry all rolled into one monstrous person. The bigger I grew with our baby, the worse my hellish life with him became.

One night, Jack came home very late. I was asleep and had a dream that our baby was choking to death. Suddenly, I awoke gasping for air. He was on top of me with a pillow over my face in an attempt to suffocate me. I fought him and somehow managed to get free. "I'm sorry. I'm drunk, honey. I didn't know what I was doing." I chalked it up to an isolated incident.

Weeks later, a horrible pain in my throat woke me up. Jack was on top of me holding a sharp butcher knife to my throat, in another attempt to kill me. I struggled with him and somehow prevailed. "What's wrong with you?"

He stormed out and didn't return until the following night.

My nightmare world with that crazy person makes me feel crazy, too. I phoned Mother about the attempts on my life. "Come home before he kills you and your unborn baby."

I grabbed my clothes and moved back into my old bedroom. Jack quickly called me. "Why did you leave? I love you."

"No you don't, or you wouldn't try to kill me and our unborn baby."

Then came a fourth call. "I promise it will never happen again." I gave in and returned to him because I believed babies need a family, and I wanted to trust him.

When I was eight months pregnant, Jack didn't like the meal I cooked for supper. He threw his plate in the trash. "I hate that food." He chased me outside with a butcher knife into the frigid night air. I ran up the dark alley toward Granny's house. In minutes, a car sped up behind me. It was Jack in our old green Hudson. He tried his best to run me down.

I swear an Angel must have carried me up that alley and helped me dodge behind a telephone pole. Otherwise, I have no idea how I outran that vehicle or managed to jump behind that telephone pole. Jack could have killed me and my unborn child that night. I was out of breath when I finally banged on Granny's back door. She flipped her back porch light on and let me inside. I stayed with her for two weeks, and he begged me to take him back again. Stupidly, I listened to him.

✳ ✳ ✳

My water broke six weeks later. After twelve hours of hard labor, we welcomed Crystal. Jack seemed pleased that we had a beautiful little girl. A month later, I was in my gown sitting on our bed bottle feeding Crystal. He attempted to grab her from my arms. "Let her finish her bottle, and then you can hold her."

"Like hell!" He grabbed Crystal and the half full glass bottle. "Get out!" He slammed the baby bottle into my thigh from across the room. It felt like a shotgun blast tore into my skin. The pain stunned me. He chased me outside into the freezing sleet and locked the door. Fury raged through me. *God please don't let him hurt Crystal.* I pounded and pounded on our door. "Let me in!"

Back in 1961, the police weren't allowed to intercede in any domestic problems. I was desperate to save Crystal. Our landlord lived next door, so I rushed to his door and told him what happened. He convinced Jack to let me back inside and take care of Crystal.

One month went by. Early one morning, Jack left for the Air Force Base. I fell asleep. Crystal was asleep in her nearby bassinet. Suddenly, Jack barged through our front door screaming like a maniac. "Where is he?"

I bolted up. "Where's who?"

"I saw your high school lover, Roland, come in the front door after I left." He scoured every inch of our small apartment.

"You must be crazy! There's no one here. I was asleep."

He grabbed Crystal and slapped me so hard in a fit of insane jealousy that he broke my jaw. I screamed in pain, fell on our bed and saw stars for the first time in my life. He went on a maniac rage. He ripped the phone out of the wall. "You'll never see your mom or high school sweetheart again. I'll kill you if you so much as try to leave this apartment."

God, who is this insane person I married? After Jack finally left for the base, I ran to a neighbor's door and phoned Momma. We moved home, and I filed for divorce. She and Harry paid for my divorce since I had no money. Six months later, Jack's blow to my jaw caused three of my front teeth to abscess on the same night. Unbearable pain woke me up. I had to endure three horrific root canals at the same time.

Within days of our divorce being final, he played on my sympathy one more time. "Baby, your church doesn't believe in divorce. They teach forgiveness and turn the other cheek. I'm sorry I hurt you. It won't happen again. I only hit you because I love you."

"Then don't love me so much."

"You have my word. It will never happen again."

Silly me, I stopped the divorce the day before it was final and returned to him one more time.

It was three months later. We went to visit his parents in Ohio. Six-month-old Crystal began to cry. He stormed toward her and screamed. "Shut up, kid, or I'll spank you."

"No, you won't spank her! Her gums are swollen. She's teething." Jack tried to spank her anyway. I rushed to stop him. We scuffled. He clutched my arm and marched me up a steep flight of stairs. On the way up, he slugged me in the middle of my back when I was half-way up the steps. I fell hard, but I managed to get up. He forced me into his mother's bedroom, locked the door and shoved me into a chair in the center of the room. I screamed for his mother to help me. She never came.

Jack glared at me like the monster he was. *"You'll never leave this room alive!"*

2

≈

No One Ever Said Life Was Fair

I screamed out to Jack's mother for many scary hours that day. "Please help me!" She totally ignored my pleas and remained downstairs. Things looked hopeless. I believed I would die in that room. A miracle happened that day. Somehow, with God's help, I managed to talk him into setting me free late that long horrific day. I moved us back home with Mother and Harry. There was no turning back. Our divorce was on. My attorney only charged me half price to refile my divorce, and then, he posed the ultimate question. *"Why did you go back to that creep?"*

"I guess it's my strict upbringing. My church taught me that divorce is a sin. That last day convinced me, if I stayed with him one more day, my days were numbered."

A job search was on the top of my list. I scoured the newspaper classifieds, heard a knock on Momma's front door and opened it. I was *not a happy camper* to see my visitors.

There stood Minister Morgan, Deacon Hayes and Elder Harris. I let them inside. Harris glared daggers at me. *"Stop this divorce right now, or you'll burn in Hell."*

"That means that you approve of Jack repeatedly trying to kill me and my baby? You can just forget it!"

Minister Morgan spoke next. "If you get a divorce you can never come to our church again."

"Our church? I thought it was *God's Church*."

Deacon Hayes put in his two cents. "Divorce is a sin in the eyes of God. You know what that means."

I stared at them in disbelief. "I'll take my chances with God, thank you. Jack is dangerous. Crystal and I lucky to be alive."

Elder Harris delivered another blow. "The Bible says that a woman must serve her husband and his needs."

"I'm getting a divorce and, frankly, I don't care if I ever set foot in *your church* again. Now it's time for you to leave."

I showed them out the door, slammed it and peered out a window. They stopped to confer on the front sidewalk and looked my way.

When Momma came home from work, I told her what happened. She quickly phoned Granny about their visit. In no time, I returned to church with Crystal. People welcomed us with open arms. Granny turned to smile at me from her pew, as we entered. I beamed. *I love my grandmother! Finally there is one person in my family who will stand up for me.*

God has a way of bringing things full circle. Three years later, those three men were the talk of the same church. The sons of the elder and deacon filed for divorce. The minister ran off with another woman. I smiled because I knew *God's Law of Karma* was at work. Even so, the church supported their sons because both dads claimed their wives had supposedly committed adultery. I know what the Bible says. "The only excuse for divorce is adultery." *I guess that death by your husband's violent hands just doesn't rate. To that I say, "Walk a mile in my shoes."*

Divorce day couldn't roll around quick enough. It felt great to be rid of Jack. His time in the Air Force ended six months later. He stopped paying child support and moved back to Ohio. He virtually vanished. I felt enormous relief.

Days later, someone at Momma's beauty shop told her about a job. I applied and went to work at our local newspaper. I could now support Crystal and myself.

One day after work, I went out back to see my lifetime companion, Smokey Joe. He appeared to be resting in a huge hole that he dug to stay cool during the hot Southern heat. I sat down on the back steps and whistled. "Come see me Smokey Joe." My Smokey didn't budge, so I went to him. He gazed up at me with his big sad eyes. He tried to stand but collapsed. I knelt beside him, stroked his head and wept.

Finally, I went inside and asked Mother to help me pick Smokey Joe up and put him in my Chevy. Bless his heart. He moaned in such pain when we lifted him. I saw gratefulness in those big sad eyes of my lifelong, best friend. It broke my heart.

Dr. Carson helped me get Smokey out of my car and into his exam room. After he finished checking Smokey, he took me to his office. He'd been Smokey's Vet for over fourteen years. I watched him shake his head. "Smokey has throat cancer. He's suffering a lot, honey. There's nothing I can do except put him down. It's the kindest thing for him."

I nodded. A sea of tears flooded my cheeks. The news was too much to bear. *I am about to lose my lifelong best friend.* I began to tremble and shake. Dr. Carson wrapped his big arms around me to comfort my loss. I hated to sign the permission slip to put Smokey Joe out of his misery. In the end, I did it for him.

I went back to tell Smokey, "Goodbye." I stroked his sweet head, gasped for air and whispered in his ear. "*Why must I put my best friend to sleep? I can't bear the thought of losing you, my sweet Smokey Joe!*"

MAY · 59

Smokey Joe – Aug '49–'63

3

≈

A New Life on the Horizon

By *March, 1965*, I met my second husband. Tim Malone was a dead ringer for actor Michael Ansara. He liked to wear a red James Dean jacket. He drove a small red car and walked somewhat stoop shouldered. I found him quite opinionated about many things, but he was a talented, moody writer. A Virgo perfectionist.

We met at work, dated, became serious and bingo. I was pregnant with my second baby. It was the same reaction from Tim. He lost interest in me, had no plans to get married and wasn't ready for a baby. I took it better this time. I had an excellent paying job and knew I could take care of Crystal and my new baby-to-be just fine.

Tim's mother, Dana Malone, would have none of it. She cornered Tim. *"You will marry Debbie.* She's carrying your child, my grandchild, and I want to be a grandmother." We had a big church wedding. Crystal was our flower girl. Our honeymoon went fine, until Tim got drunk and passed out. I quickly realized I had married a seriously out-of-control alcoholic who feared any form of responsibility, especially if it involved a decision of any kind. *What is it with me and alcoholics?*

Stacy Malone entered the world on *St. Patrick's Day in 1966.* Life with Tim seemed good, until Tim resumed drinking. Apparently, he had many fears that included the responsibility of children, yet I believed we could be a happy healthy family. In time, Tim agreed to adopt Crystal.

Soon, an old nemesis reared its ugly head. Tim's drinking escalated every week. I tried repeatedly to encourage him to see a counselor, join an AA group or both. I wanted things to work out, until Tim began to have blackouts. He would go missing for days at a time. His drinking sucked up every penny we needed for our bills and food, even with both of us working.

In *September of 1969*, the last straw broke. Tim went missing for five days. I called every nearby hospital. He eventually stumbled in our back door early one morning. I heard him throw up in the hallway, so I jumped out of bed. He wobbled past me to our bedroom all bleary-eyed. He left a trail of smelly clothes and fell on our bed with a sick moan.

I cleaned up his hallway carpet mess, tossed his soiled clothes in the washer and returned to bed. I no sooner fell asleep than he wet the bed so bad it drenched our mattress. Then I realized his urine had also soaked my pajamas. I jumped up and changed clothes. Come morning, Tim wobbled into our kitchen with blood-shot eyes. I couldn't stand to look at him anymore. I sat on my kitchen counter in complete frustration. "I want a divorce, and I want you to move today."

"I don't want a divorce."

"Well I do. I can't take your drinking, blackouts and going missing for days on end. I looked everywhere for you. The kids and I can't live like this."

"Please don't do this. It won't happen again. I promise." *I've heard those words too many times before in my life.* "You say that every time. Last night was the last straw. It's over." Despite Tim's tearful pleas, I filed for divorce. His revenge was swift. He moved a half block away into an apartment.

My greatest heartbreak came when I put both of my kids in *Little Ones Day Care*. Stacy was in their pre-school. Their bus took Crystal to Grade School every day. Tim took them for a weekend visit shortly after our divorce was final. When he dropped them off at Little Ones on Monday morning, there was a scene.

Mrs. Janski, a sweet Polish woman with a pockmarked face, ran Little Ones. As I picked up the kids, she met me outside the front door in tears. "I must share what happened this morning. When Tim dropped off Crystal and Stacy and turned to leave. Little Stacy raced after him and threw his arms around his legs. 'Don't go, Daddy! No!' The sight of that sweet boy grieving like that almost ripped out my heart."

Tears welled up in my eyes. I put my hand over my mouth for a moment. "I had no choice. Tim's drinking was out of control. I couldn't take it anymore."

She hugged me, and we went inside to get my kids. Crystal seemed fine, but Stacy looked so sad that day. I knew he was hurting inside. It grieved my heart to see it. Things with Stacy rapidly went from bad to worse. A few months later, Mrs. Janski met me outside again. "My sweet little Stacy hit a girl in the head with a toy radio today. She had to get several stitches."

I dropped my head. "Oh no!"

After that I did my best to give Stacy lots of extra attention. Momma and Harry came to visit one day. We went outside to sit around the pool and visit. Suddenly, Crystal screamed bloody murder, and so did Mother. I turned to see what had happened. Stacy bit Crystal's cheek so hard that it left deep teeth imprints on her.

Momma snapped. "What are you going to do about this?"

Harry growled. "Yeah, look at poor Crystal's face."

"What do you want me to do? He's only four."

Harry growled. "Well do something."

I didn't know what to do. In sheer frustration, I bit Stacy on his cheek. *Oh great!* Now both kids are crying. I feel like a monster. I was sick at my stomach. After that incident, Stacy never bit anyone else. It wasn't long before he hurt another small boy at Little Ones. Mrs. Janski pulled me aside. "I have to ask you to find another school for Stacy." And so, I did.

✳ ✳ ✳

Our divorce was final on *Nov. 30, 1969.* I accepted a date with Mike Williams. Tim spied on us the whole evening. When Mike walked me to my door, I heard my phone ringing and went inside to answer it. A deafening voice shot through my telephone line. "Get that son-of-a-bitch out of my house right now!"

"This isn't your house. I bought you out in our divorce. My dating life is none of your business."

On *June 13, 1970,* I married my third husband. Bart Austin was barely taller than me. He had hazel eyes, an arched nose, high IQ and mega confidence. His warm brown hair looked *JFK perfect.* He oozed charm, was more confident than Tim, and much kinder than Jack. I was smooth crazy about him. I knew he was an ex-con, but he served his time for burglarizing a bank and was out on parole. He convinced me he was a changed man. *Bart's the most charming man I ever met.* I bet he can sell fried ice cream to anyone. He's a true cowboy from head-to-toe, and he smokes a lot.

Crystal instantly hit it off with Bart and his son, Darren. He and Stacy promptly disliked each other. During Darren's every-other-weekend visits, he and Stacy had occasional squabbles. I remained optimistic that things would work out.

She was eight, Darren was six and Stacy's four. I presume they leave Stacy out of their fun due to his young age.

✵ ✵ ✵

Tim didn't help matters. He continually created friction with me, and he used Crystal and Stacy to do it. One of the worst occasions was the day he took them for the weekend. He still lived a half block from our house. Two hours later, Crystal phoned me. "Tim passed out drunk. We're bored. Can we come home?"

"Of course. Start walking home. I'll meet you half-way." I hung up, went out our back door and met them down the street. In no time, our phone rang.

"Why did you come get the kids?"

"They asked to come home because you passed out. I told them to walk home and met them half-way."

"I'm coming to get them."

"No, you aren't. I don't want them around you, when you're drinking." He slammed his phone in my ear.

Shortly, someone pounded on our patio door. It was Tim. I slid the glass door open slightly. "Your visit's over. Go home!"

"Bitch! I'll get them one way or the other!" He grabbed the door and tried to force his way inside. I screamed.

Bart pushed past me faster than lightning and backed Tim down the steps. "Lay a hand on her, and you'll answer to me."

Tim was belligerent and swung at Bart. *A big mistake.* Bart whipped out his pocketknife and cut Tim's stomach three times. Blood spots appeared on Tim's shirt. "You son-of-a-bitch! You cut me, you motherfucker! The police will arrest you."

"Get out of here, or I'll do it again."

Tim went home and called the police. Two policemen knocked on our door. Bart opened it. "Mr. Austin, you're under arrest." They handcuffed him.

I interceded. "What are you doing? He was protecting me from Tim. He was drunk and barged in the back door after me!"

"Ma'am, if you don't stop yelling, I'll arrest you, too."

On Monday, I called Jerry Kahn, Bart's long-time attorney and explained what happened. He phoned the police station and called me back. "I can get Bart released, but someone has to back his twenty-five-thousand-dollar bond."

"Whoa! We don't have that kind of money. Let me call his Uncle Fred." Bart's one lucky guy. Fred and Jennifer used their home as collateral to cover Bart's enormous bond.

Jerry had Bart released from jail in one hour. Since Bart was still on parole, his parole officer cut down on his freedoms, and that was the end of it.

And then, Tim and his family used the incident to brand Bart as a dangerous person. They repeatedly bad-mouthed him to my kids. Tim even told his family and my children a big whopping fib. He claimed that I had an affair with Bart during our marriage. Crystal came home and told me all about it.

I was furious. "Honey, that's the biggest lie I've ever heard. Bart made a few passes at me, before he went to prison for burglary. He always heard my standard answer. "No." Our divorce was final four months before anyone even dreamed Bart might get released from prison a year early. He only served one year."

Even though my marriage to Bart had some rough spots, it was also some of my happiest times. Sadly, he invariably managed to be fired by every employer he had during our marriage. One of the worst times was when he hit a co-worker in the head with a piece of sidebar at a newspaper. He swore it was an accident. They still fired him anyway. I wanted to believe him. I found it to be a stretch. Since we were working at the same company, I was too embarrassed to go to work for two weeks after his incident.

Five years later on Valentine's Day and against my pleas, Bart tried to steal a railroad car full of paper to sell it. His buyers turned out to be undercover policemen. That stupid stunt landed him in jail again. I phoned Jerry. He saved Bart's butt one more time.

✲ ✲ ✲

When summer arrived, friction erupted between Stacy and Darren during a weekend visit. Bart was at work. Darren seemed to intentionally knock Stacy off our tall pool ladder. He pushed past him to be the first one down the slide. Stacy flew into a giant rosebush and came up bloody and screaming. I saw the incident and dashed to help my son. Darren kept right on swimming, as if nothing had occurred. *Amazing...*

I took Stacy inside to doctor his wounds and put him on his bed to rest. Then I returned outside. "Darren, get out of the pool and come inside." No way would I spank him, so I put him on Crystal's bed until Bart came home.

Crystal didn't sure what to do, so she came in the house and watched TV. Hours later, Bart came bopping in our back door all smiles and kissed me. "Where's Darren?"

"There was a problem, so I put him on Crystal's bed until you came home." I could almost see steam shooting from his ears. He wheeled around, hurried to see Darren, gathered his clothes and drove him home without a word. *A bad feeling hit my mind. I could sense that Bart's silence was a brewing storm.*

He stayed gone for the longest time. When he returned home, things rapidly went south between us. Little indiscretions began to pop up. One weekend, he flopped on a kitchen chair with a worried look. "My doctor says that I'm going to die before Crystal graduates. I have a serious heart problem. I need some time to be alone and think."

His news overwhelmed me. *I love Bart. I don't want to be a widow.* A few days later, he returned home. He never told me where he went. He did this more than once.

Out of the blue came a heartbreaking phone call from Momma. "Honey, Granny passed away today."

I burst into tears. "No! She can't die!" Bart was nowhere to be found for when I needed him the most. He finally showed up days later. "Granny died two days ago. Her funeral is tomorrow."

He hugged me. "I'm not able to go to her funeral."

"Why not?"

"Here I am, unsure of how many breaths I have left to live another day. You and the kids go without me."

My brother, Matt, flew in for the funeral. He could tell I was a basket case. I couldn't stop crying. "Sis, you've got to pull yourself together."

"You don't understand. Granny died only days after Bart told me he won't live to see Crystal graduate."

✳ ✳ ✳

Matt and I sat on the front row beside Momma at Granny's funeral. My tears flowed endlessly, as I grieved for her and for Bart's failing health. He helped me up and walked me toward Granny's casket. I could hear myself weeping and wailing. Everyone else in the funeral home could hear me, too. I was inconsolable.

Matt hugged me and walked me out a side door. "You've must get hold of yourself. We're all hurting today."

"I know, but I can't. This isn't right!" The rest of the day was a blur. I stayed in Mother's black car at the cemetery. No way could I watch my Granny be buried in the ground.

Weeks passed. Bart still refused to talk about his health. One hot Saturday in June, I took Crystal and Stacy to a movie. Afterward, I parked in our back driveway. We walked to the back cement stairs to our patio sliding glass door. I was unprepared for the sight of finding Bart sprawled out on our back steps in his swimsuit. I was horrified to see him clutching his chest and gasping for air. I became hysterical. "What can I do? What's happening to you?"

He gasped in a weak voice. "It's my heart. Get my pills."

"Where are they?"

"Look in my jeans pocket."

I grabbed his jeans from a lawn chair by the pool and retrieved his pills. I was a basket case as I opened the bottle and gave him a small pill. He put it under his tongue. I watched his eyes seem to roll back in his head. "I'm taking you to the hospital!"

"No, I'll be fine in a minute." He rallied slowly and sat up clutching his chest. The incident scared me to death. When Bart was able to stand, I helped him inside our house.

"It's time you tell me what's going on."

"My doctor says that my heart muscle is weak. I have angina. I could die at any moment."

After that day, Bart's angina attacks increased. I'd find him in his truck or in our hallway clutching his heart.

I am a complete basket case. I dearly love Bart. Why has life dumped so much stress on me at one time?

✷ ✷ ✷

Three months later, Lori Holland, one of my more talkative girlfriends who worked with Bart, phoned me.

"Debbie, why don't you drop by at suppertime and pay Bart a surprise visit sometime?"

"Why should I do that?"

"I'd rather not say. I just think you need to do it."

Her request whirred in my head, so I took Stacy and Crystal with me to Bart's workplace. She saw us walk in and hurried over. "Bart went out to eat with... *a friend.*"

"What friend?"

"Her name is Evelyn."

The kids and I sat on a bench and waited in the lobby for Bart and his *friend* to return. Lori scurried back to work. Shortly, I heard Bart's boots echoing down the hallway. He and his red-headed friend sashayed through the door giggling. She saw me and dashed to work. He was all nervous grins, as he approached and sat beside me. "What are you doing here, goodlookin'?"

"What are you doing with her is the better question."

He shrugged. "She's new and hated to eat alone."

"Is that a fact?"

"Honest Injun!" He shrugged with a flirty grin.

I wanted to believe him, until I noticed he was suddenly wearing sexy underwear and cologne. *Funny thing. He always tells me that cologne makes him sick.*

When Bart was in the shower, I opened his wallet and found his lonely friend's photo along with her name and telephone number. Apparently, she was a *not so lonely redhead named Evelyn Stone.*

One night, Bart never come home after work. I woke up about three a.m. He still wasn't there. I tossed and turned for hours. Finally, I woke up, dressed and drove to work, but I couldn't concentrate. I felt confident he was with Evelyn, so I asked to leave work, phoned Bart's boss for her address east of town and drove there to find them.

I knew everything except her apartment number. I parked beside Bart's Blazer Chalet, grabbed my glass pop bottle and began pounding on various doors with my bottle. I was in search of Evelyn Stone's whereabouts.

From out of nowhere, Bart approached me in the parking lot. "We heard a shrill voice and banging. Evelyn looked out her upstairs window. She turned white as a sheet, when she saw you."

"It's too bad I didn't find her. Where's her apartment?"

"I don't want a scene."

"Let's go home."

"Are you sure?"

"You're my husband not hers." In hindsight, I wish I had left his butt at her apartment that day. Silly me, I wanted him back. He was my husband, and I still loved him.

When we arrived at home, he walked straight to our bathroom to comb his perfectly shaped brown hair. I followed him to the door. He stared into the mirror, slowly combed his hair and spoke in the most sarcastic tone. *"You wanted me. You got me."*

They say love is blind. Unfortunately, I'm living proof of it. Things quickly subsided at home. Before long, Bart offered to coach Stacy's baseball team. That seemed like a positive sign. Since I was a tomboy in grade school and played baseball and football, I was happy that Stacy showed an interest in sports. It wasn't long before it was clear that Stacy had no interest in baseball. He became the team benchwarmer. Bart catered to the boys who showed more interest. Stacy occasionally played centerfield or batted. Those times were rare.

One thing became too commonplace, Bart's friendship with a scorekeeper named Marty Brooks. She often came to our house for a swim, when Bart was there alone.

Crystal approached Bart one evening in our den. "Dad, I want you to be an assistant coach on my softball team because I want to play catcher."

"Okay, if you let me teach you how to tag the runners so you won't get hurt."

"That's fine with me." Crystal grinned. They spent lots of time together at a local park, so he could show her how to play catcher and not be injured.

I was pleasantly surprised, when Crystal showed real talent as a catcher. Her team eventually made the playoffs. Stacy would wander off during her games and play on the park swings.

My life slowly returned to a happy level. Bart sometimes surprised me. We'd go grocery shopping together, hold hands and skip down the aisles like young lovers once again.

✳ ✳ ✳

Bart's boss moved him to the night shift at work. I worked days at my job. He drove the kids to school, and I picked them up after my work day ended. Not ideal for a married couple, but we had no choice. We often passed each other on the freeway going opposite directions and waved at each other.

✳ ✳ ✳

One summer day, I answered our den phone. "Yes, this is Mrs. Austin... I'll send my husband right away." I turned to Bart in a panic. "Crystal's in trouble. She and her girlfriend, Paulla Sanders, are at the Seven-Eleven at the top of the hill. The manager wants one of us there right away."

"I'll take care of it." He dashed out the door. I was a nervous wreck, until they returned. He grabbed her arm as they walked inside.

"You're getting a spanking. I'm grounding you for six weeks." She swelled up and stomped to our master bedroom.

"What happened?"

"The girls were caught shoplifting candy, cigarettes and stuff, and the store manager called the police. Officer Lewis showed up, handcuffed them and put them in his squad car to put the fear of God into them. He said that it might stop them from doing it again. I convinced the manager not to press charges."

"Why on earth would Crystal shoplift? We give her a nice allowance every week?"

He shrugged. "Who knows?" He walked down the hall and closed our bedroom door. I heard Crystal yell, each time his belt hit her.

Bart always favored Crystal, so it really surprised me when he spanked her for shoplifting. I felt sorry for her because they were so close. Tim had adopted her. Sadly, they never bonded.

※ ※ ※

After Crystal turned fourteen, we drove to my hometown for a short visit. She pouted the whole trip because she wanted to stay home with her boyfriend, Bobby Jones. When we arrived to see Pop Sherman, Crystal refused to get out. He was now in his early nineties and was never a big talker. He liked to recall his time in the Spanish-American War, and he now walked with a cane. Granny had passed away two years earlier, after she broke her hip. Mother finally arrived and joined us. Pop Sherman looked around the room and frowned. "Where's Crystal?"

I shook my head. "Pouting in the truck. Sweetheart, will you go get her?"

"Sure will." Bart left and returned with Crystal, but she remained extremely sullen. He sat her on his lap and tickled her to improve her mood. I even took their picture.

I knelt by Pop Sherman. "How are you feeling today?"

"Tolerable."

I watched him look at Crystal. "How's school young lady?" She was giggling so loud from Bart's tickling that she failed to respond to him. He turned to Stacy. "How are you doing?"

"I caught a bunch of fish in the Heritage Park pond last week." The two of them had a nice discussion about fishing, until it was time to end our visit.

A month passed by. Mother and Harry came to our home for a visit. She asked me to drive her to the grocery store. On our return trip, she surprised me. "Pop Sherman doesn't want Bart in his home ever again."

I couldn't believe my ears. "Why would he say that?"

"He didn't like the way Bart touched Crystal. It's not how a parent should touch a child."

"I was there. I saw nothing wrong. He tickled her."

"He thinks Bart's too friendly with Crystal."

"That's ridiculous. He was kidding around with her like any dad would do. He was trying to get her over her ugly mood."

"Harry and I feel the same way about Bart."

"He wasn't even at Pop Sherman's that day. Besides, he's one to talk. He only liked me when he was drunk and hated me when he was sober. This is some kind of crazy talk!"

"Bart was way out of line."

"I've never seen Bart do anything to Crystal that I thought was inappropriate. *If I had, I would be the first one to say something.*

You know me, Mother. I don't mince words." I tuned out the rest of Mother's rant and avoided seeing them for a long time after that.

✳ ✳ ✳

Bart surprised me with the oddest gift that Christmas morning. He gave me a red belly dance outfit from Frederick's of Hollywood. I looked at him with curiosity. "What am I supposed to do with this?"

"Our neighbor, Beulah Bland, needs someone to take belly dance lessons with her at the recreation center. I want you to try it."

I shook my head. "You know I never learned how to dance. Our church wouldn't allow it."

"Baby, you're now in a Baptist Church that's more tolerant."

"Why not return my gift to the store? I can't do it."

"Goodlookin', I want you to *do it for me.*"

Crystal and Stacy were all ears to our conversation. Bart leaned close and whispered. "Kitten, it is time you learned how to dance. Surprise me!"

Days later, Beulah paid me a surprise visit. She was a stern-faced older woman with a semi-pockmarked face and a haughty attitude that wouldn't quit.

✳ ✳ ✳

Beulah was not my favorite neighbor. Years earlier, she told her son, Todd, to slug Stacy in the stomach after they had an argument. Stacy was only six at the time. He came home crying and told me what had happened. I stormed to her door and banged on it until she answered. "That better not ever happen again, or this is between you and me!" She slammed her door in my face.

✳ ✳ ✳

In spite of that incident, Bart liked Beulah for some odd reason. *Now she's in our hallway asking me to take belly dance lessons with her? Go figure.*

"Bart tells me you're ready to take some lessons."

"I don't know about that."

"Come on, Debbie. It'll be lots of fun." I finally gave in and agreed. She lasted all of two weeks. "Belly dancing is too hard for me. I plan to drop out."

"I'm finally learning how to dance, so want to stay in class." I practiced almost every night at home. My belly dancing skills improved weekly.

✳ ✳ ✳

Years later, *Stacy still talks about hearing my zeals and the Greek music* playing late at night when I practiced my dancing.

✳ ✳ ✳

I eventually let Bart watch me dance. He was ultra-turned on. It pleased me that he liked my dancing. In time, I wanted to improve my dancing skills. I signed up for advance lessons with an instructor named Angelica. A classmate, Sondra Jackson, and I took turns driving to-and-from the new lessons. Bart offered to entertain Stacy and Crystal on the nights I took my new lessons.

One fall night months later, Sondra drove me to class. We found a note on the door. *No class tonight due to an emergency.* On the way home, I told Sondra about an incident with Stacy's teacher earlier that day.

"Would you believe Stacy's second grade teacher called me in for a teacher's conference. She asked me to change his name and said that the kids make fun of him because he has a girl's name. Plus, he gets into fights every day. She even had the nerve to talk to him about choosing another name."

"How dreadful."

"I'll say. I named him after a dear friend who tragically died in a car accident. Besides, lots of names are interchangeable for a boy or a girl."

"What did your son say about it?"

"I wrote him a poem about why his name is special. I even mentioned famous actors also named Stacy and I told him that I loved him very much. Then I made it into a plaque."

"I bet that made him feel a lot better."

"I hope so. I hung it on his bedroom wall."

Sondra dropped me off at home. I hurried inside and walked toward our bedroom. I saw our black light glowing from our door. I turned the corner and froze.

I don't recall breathing for several minutes. I saw the shock of my life, right before my eyes...

Debbie & Bart's Bedroom

4

≈

Snake Charmer Alert

I stared at Bart's outline underneath the sheets of our king-sized bed. A giggling female lay beside him. Words finally rolled across my numb lips. *"What the hell's going on here?"*

The sheets flew back. I watched in shock. My nude fifteen-year-old daughter jumped up and scampered past me to her room. I slammed the door and glared at Bart. "How could you?"

"This is not what you think."

"You lying snake!"

"I swear on a stack of Bibles. We were smoking pot but nothing more. This has never happened before. It was a mistake. I promise it won't be repeated. Come on. Weed makes people do stupid things. This was stupid, yet innocent."

I was furious. My head felt as if it was about to explode, and the breath had been knocked out of me. *How could this happen? Betrayal coursed through my veins. My heart wanted to believe him. My head was dubious.* I was inconsolable.

Bart pleaded and cried. "On my life this never happened before tonight. You know I'm crazy about you, baby. I am so sorry."

Eventually, he convinced me that the villain was their pot smoking because it impaired one's better judgment. He reminded me that *forgiveness was the Christian thing to do, so I forgave them. I say them, since Crystal was old enough to know better.*

Mr. Snake Charmer quickly shot into high gear. I received flowers and candy on a regular basis. Many gifts arrived from Frederick's of Hollywood every week. He even arranged a one week vacation for us to fly to Puerto Vallarta. It was our first trip without the kids. We had a heavenly time, until I became badly sunburned. I looked like a red lobster the day we flew home.

✳ ✳ ✳

Months later, my longtime friend with a strong Southern drawl, Adelle Brady, called me at home. "Debbie, I think you need to check on Crystal during her lunch time at school."

"Why should I do that?"

"Every day she gives her lunch money to her boyfriend and goes without food."

"How would you know that?"

"My granddaughter goes to her school and sees her do it."

"I will check it out."

I discussed it with Bart. He agreed to handle it. On Thursday morning, he drove to Crystal's school and watched her from a distance. She gave Bobby her lunch money.

Bart greeted me, as I walked to our front porch after work. "Adelle was right about Crystal, so I brought her home and grounded her for two weeks."

I frowned. "Can this be why she tried to shoplift? She needed food at school."

"Nah. I doubt they're related."

When her grounding was over, Crystal found me in the kitchen. "Mom, can I go to Bobby's house? He offered to help me with my homework."

It sounded harmless. "Okay. Be home by six." Six p.m. arrived. There was no Crystal in sight. I walked outside, saw one of her classmates named Harley Huff amble past our house. I stopped him. "Have you seen Crystal today?"

"She's still at Bobby's house."

"And still doing homework?"

He couldn't look me in the eye. "She can't come home."

"Why is that?"

He walked away, and I grabbed his arm. "I want the truth."

"He offered us some drugs. Crystal is real sick."

Please God, I don't want to lose my daughter to drugs.

I rushed inside to find Bart and told him what Mike said. He dashed to his truck and stayed gone for the longest time. Finally, he brought Crystal home. She went to her room without a word. I turned to Bart. "What happened?"

"Bobby gave her some *dusted drugs.* She'll be fine, but I told her, 'No more Bobby.' She needs to sleep it off."

I walked into her room when she woke up. "About Bobby..."

She bolted up, clutched her pillow and began to screech at me like a wild banshee. "I won't stop seeing Bobby. I love him. You can't keep me away from him!"

"I am your mother, and I will stop you! No one gives my daughter drugs that could kill her."

Crystal hurriedly learned that I kept my word. We did keep her away from Bobby. We grounded her for two months and monitored her whereabouts when she wasn't at school. Bobby and his family unexpectedly moved to another town shortly afterward. My mind often wondered if Bart had something to do with their super sudden departure. Fearing his answer, I never asked him about it.

✱✱✱

Meanwhile, Stacy's fifth grade teacher began to phone me every day or so to complain about his bad behavior. My response never wavered. "I expect you to control him at school. He gets plenty of discipline at home. He would never get away with the things here that he does in your classroom." Her calls increased in volume for months, with complaint after complaint. Finally, I had enough. "Just spank him."

"Oh no. I can't do that."

"I give you permission to do it."

"I won't spank him." His teacher remained adamant. She refused to discipline Stacy and continued to call me for weeks to complain. In total frustration, I approached Bart. "I hear the same thing every year with all of Stacy's teachers. They refuse to make him mind, but they regularly call me to complain about him. Would you go to his class and give him a spanking in front of his classmates?"

"Are you sure?"

"When I was in the first grade, twelve of us kids were caught throwing erasers during lunchtime. Our teacher called us in front of the class one-at-a-time and spanked us with a ruler. It completely humiliated me. I promised myself I'd behave because I never wanted to be that shamed again. It worked for me. *Just maybe it will work on Stacy."*

Stacy's spanking at school seemed to help for a short time. Only months later, I was halfway through a twelve-week cake decorating class at a nearby mall. Bart usually came home from work an hour after I left for class. That Saturday, I drove to the mall. I was excited we were going to decorate a wedding cake. After class, I parked in our back driveway.

Bart was leaning on his truck with a worried look as I stepped out of my car. "I need to explain everything before you go inside. Something happened and..." My heart sank. I tried to rush past him. He gripped my arms to stop me. "It is not as bad as you think. *Everyone is safe. The fire is totally out.*"

✳ ✳ ✳

The moment I heard *the word fire*, my mind raced back in time to a day I was five-years-old. My dad was still living with us. My brother, Matt Curtis, had joined the Air Force to get away from him and his cruelty. We were very poor and lived in a small shotgun house. *It means that a shotgun blast can fly through the front door, head straight thru the house and exit the back door.*

Shotgun House Burned Down

It was a biting cold day that gave me my first sight of an ice storm. The neighborhood resembled a winter wonderland full of icicles. My dad had given me a little black puppy for Christmas. It was my first dog. Momma had received an invitation to a nearby neighbor's house to attend a Tupperware party. Our small house had limited heat, so she put my puppy in our tiny bathroom on a rug and lit a small gas heater on the floor with a match to keep my puppy warm.

After the party was underway, I remember hearing lots of sirens echoing in the crisp, outside air. Mother dashed toward me with my coat and hat. In minutes, she was pulling me across the slick icy yards toward our home. I saw rolls of billowing black smoke shooting from our roof. My thoughts raced to my little puppy trapped inside. Tears rolled down my *frozen cheeks*. Momma screamed and cried. I stood on our icy yard and watched in horror as she mounted the steep cement stairs and grabbed the front doorknob.

The moment she opened the door, a huge arm of black smoke shot out and engulfed her. Flames began to dance on the tips of her short brown hair. She wailed. "Help me!" Then she raced down the steps and ran in circles on our yard.

"Someone help my Mommy!" I had no idea what to do. Luckily, the fire trucks arrived. A fireman jumped off their firetruck, grabbed her and wrapped a wet towel around her hair to put out the flames.

In my young mind, I thought the firemen would take over, put the fire out, and things would be fine. Instead, Momma fought to get free from the fireman and rushed back inside our burning home. I was numb with fear. When she carried a chair out the door, dropped it on the ground and rushed back into the fire, I cringed. *Is Momma going to die?*

After the firemen had the flames under control, the same fireman who saved Momma handed me my badly singed teddy bear and two dolls. That was all I had left from the inferno. I gazed up at him. "Have you seen my little puppy?"

His eyes grew sad. "Your little guy went to Puppy Heaven."

When I went to bed at Granny's house that night, an old nightmare, that had paralyzed me with fear since I was two-years-old, returned. *A raging elephant or a screaming gorilla would chase me down our dusty street.* I always ran for my life for blocks and blocks from one of the giant animals, in my dream.

✳ ✳ ✳

Bart shook my arm. Those horrid memories left me as quickly as they came. I tried to rush past him again. "Were the kids hurt?"

He blocked my path. "They are going to be fine, but our new couch is on the patio and..."

I pushed past him and raced to our patio. My heart broke when I saw gutted holes filled with black soot scattered across our blue sectional couch. Bart followed me. I turned to him. "How did the fire start?"

"Apparently, Stacy was sitting on the couch flicking one of my old lighters underneath the macramé hanger you just made. A fireman told me that macramé is extremely flammable. In seconds, it went up in flames. Stacy became frantic and ran to Beulah's house for help. Crystal was washing her hair, smelled smoke, ran to the den and tried to put the fire out with her wet towel. Her hair and eyelashes are badly singed, even so, she's doing okay."

My head reeled. All I could think of was how Crystal and Stacy could have died just like Mother almost did years ago.

When I entered our patio door that nauseating house fire smell hit me in the face. *It is the same unique odor one never forgets the rest of your life, after your home burns down.*

Clusters of burn spots covered our new vinyl floor in the kitchen and den. Every wall of the house had smoke damage. I completely lost it. I took Bart's belt from his jeans, chased Stacy to his room and gave him a whipping. The whole fire incident was very Traumatic. It took me weeks to get over how close I came to losing Stacy, Crystal and another home in a dreadful house fire.

✳ ✳ ✳

Suddenly, someone touched my shoulder. I looked up to see the stewardess pause beside my row with her drink cart. "Would you like something to drink?"

I closed my book and nodded. "Yes. I need an Amaretto and Coke on the rocks."

She handed me my drink and noticed the book in my lap. "What do you think?"

"Think about what?"

"Will it be the boy or the girl who becomes a porn star?"

"Have you read the book?"

"I bought it last week and just finished Chapter Five."

"Which child are you leaning toward?"

"The boy is always in trouble and is quite rebellious."

"True, but the girl is desperately in search of love and attention. She isn't exactly an angel."

"I guess time will tell." She smiled and pushed her cart down the aisle to serve other passengers.

I sipped my drink and stared out the window at the night sky. Minutes later, I resumed reading Debbie Austin's story...

✳ ✳ ✳

Things grew worse and worse between Stacy and Bart. I guess it was predictable, given that Darren was no longer visiting with us. I also faced the ordeal of working out a settlement with the insurance company over the fire loss estimate and handling the repair work that followed. It took six weeks to get our home back to normal and totally remove that horrid smell.

A month passed by. I came home late from my cake decorating class and entered the house. I peered into Stacy's room. He was on his bed. I could see that his eyes were red from crying. "Is something wrong, honey?"

"Bart became mad, hit me with my trash can and almost broke my arm because I might..."

Out of nowhere, Bart walked up behind me and interrupted. "He talked back to me, when I told him to do something."

"I won't have you batter Stacy with a trash can. Hurting him won't cut it with me."

"You're right. I lost my temper. It won't happen again."

I sat beside Stacy to check on his swollen forearm. "I am going to put some castor oil and a heating pad on your arm to help the swelling go down."

✳ ✳ ✳

I decided to search for a boy's private Catholic School, and I enrolled Stacy in their sixth grade. I read that Catholic Priests were quite strict and can work wonders with troubled boys. *It certainly didn't hurt to hope.* After the first semester ended, I received a call from Father Tim. "Mrs. Austin, can you come in for a progress report on Stacy?"

When I arrived, Father Tim began. "I am afraid we are unable to manage Stacy or his behavior problems. We want you to find another school for him. He doesn't fit in here."

I almost choked. "I thought if anyone could handle him it would be your school."

Father Tim shook his head and walked me to the door. "Good luck, Mrs. Austin."

Stacy was waiting outside. I drove him home and notified the public school that he would be returning the next semester. He completed the sixth grade in public school. I could only hope that middle school would be a new start for him.

In short order, I received a call the first month from yet another teacher about Stacy's conduct. "Mrs. Austin, Stacy knocked my calculator off the desk and broke it. Please come pick him up. I expelled him for two weeks." *Here we go again.*

Bart drove to the school and visited with the teacher. This time, his charm failed to convince her to allow Stacy to remain in school. Stacy was expelled. When they returned home, they had heated words in the hallway. Bart yanked off his belt, and he spanked him too hard and too long. I raced from the kitchen. "Stop it right now! That is enough!"

He growled at me. "Stay out of it!"

"He's my son. I will never stay out of it."

I grabbed for Bart's belt as he swung it toward Stacy. He wheeled toward me with a hateful glare. It was a look I was totally unaccustomed to seeing in his hazel eyes. His cold demeanor reminded me of my daddy. He slung the belt aside and stormed to the den for a smoke. We barely spoke the rest of the day. Stacy stayed on his bed, talked on the phone and was unusually quiet until bedtime.

After two weeks, Stacy prepared to return to school. I saw him briefly before I left for work. Bart told me later that Stacy had met him at the front door. "I want to ride my skateboard to school today."

When I drove home from work that afternoon, Crystal met me at the door. "Mom, someone was calling for you."

The phone rang. I grabbed it. "Hello?"

I heard a strange voice on the line. "Stacy's not in school today. Is he sick?"

"No, he should be there."

"We have not seen him all day."

I was later informed by my attorney that Stacy had called Tim regarding Bart's whippings and the trash can incident. Tim gave Stacy instructions. "Come to my apartment on Monday morning, instead of school." Stacy did as Tim said. Then he spirited him to an airport, flew him out of state and hid him.

Tim's court filing by his attorney was stern. "Bart was being physically abusive to Stacy."

School Superintendent Clark called me the following day and requested a meeting in his office. Bart went with me. We sat across from Mr. Clark. "Mrs. Austin, per School District rules we will fine you five-hundred-dollars a day, until you get Stacy back in school." I nearly fell out of the chair. Bart slammed his fist on Clark's desk and scared him.

I stood up. "How can I return Stacy to school? I have no idea where he is since his father kidnapped him."

"That is not my problem. *That is your problem.*"

It was obvious that Superintendent Clark had little concern for my son's welfare. His main agenda revolved around money the School District would lose for each day of his absence. He refused to be reasonable, so we left.

Bart dropped me off at home and drove to work. I walked inside and found Crystal. "Honey, I want you to phone Dana's boyfriend, Brian. He may know where Tim hid Stacy."

When Brian answered the phone, he innocently let the cat out of the bag to Crystal. "Yeah, Stacy's staying with Dana."

"Crystal, now call Dana and see who answers."

She dialed Dana's number. Stacy answered. "Hello."

"When are you coming home? Mom is upset that you're gone."

"I'm going to enroll in school and stay here."

The entire incident was heart wrenching, and the significant court costs were a financial burden. Greg Long was my attorney. He filed a Court Injunction to force Tim to return Stacy to our state. The hearing was long and stressful. Finally, we reached an agreement in the hallway with our lawyer's input. We agreed on Joint Custody. It was new by legal standards in the eighties. It meant Stacy could choose to live with Tim or me because of his age.

Melvin Jones was Tim's attorney. He approached me in the hall. "Stacy wants to live with Tim. He will call me, when he's ready to visit you." Those words hurt like hell. I fought back tears.

"If he prefers to live with an alcoholic, he can see what I put up with for almost five years. Yes, I accept Stacy's decision." The attorneys returned to the Judge Chambers and set up a Court Order for Joint Custody of Stacy. The whole process emotionally drained me. When I came home, I took one look at his empty room and wept at his doorway. It was a hard realization that my son wasn't coming home. I cried myself to sleep that night.

✳ ✳ ✳

Unexpectedly, my boss, Mr. Gordon, posted a note on the employee bulletin board. "Only management personnel can park on the company lot." *Oh great, now where can I park and be safe?* I found a building to park inside about five blocks away.

I received a list from Melvin's office about the items Stacy wants sent to Tim's apartment. *It devastated me to pack his belongings into boxes.* I felt he was gone forever.

Within the hour, Greg phoned. "I was just notified me that Tim rented a house. His mother is moving here to help take care of Stacy."

"That is just great. Tim works two jobs, so I guess Dana can have her turn at trying to handle Stacy."

"Maybe it's for the best, Debbie."

"She's also an alcoholic. My boy doesn't stand *a snowball's chance in hell over there.*" I hung up and tried to keep my mind occupied. It was a struggle to stay positive that day. I shut Stacy's door to avoid looking at his empty room.

✳ ✳ ✳

Bart walked into our den a week later with a gun he wanted to clean. He always kept a few guns in his closet for security. "I wish you wouldn't bring that in here. You guns scare me."

"Baby, it is not loaded." He sat on the couch, opened the Magnum's bullet chamber and whirled it. "The chamber's empty."

"I don't care. Guns make me nervous. I don't want to be around them."

"You can hold the bullets while I clean the gun."

I shook my head and went to bed early. I had no idea that irony was perched on my horizon ready to raise its ugly head again.

The day was *Saturday, June 23, 1980.* A warm sun was shining on the downtown warehouse district as I left work. I walked four blocks to a locked parking building where I now parked my car. When I backed my Firebird into the deserted street, I lowered my electric window slightly to let in some fresh air.

Debbie's Car

Out of nowhere, a young Mexican male in a white t-shirt and jeans rushed to my window. "Hey lady. Do you know where Harley Street is?" Then he pointed east. I looked in that direction. When I turned back, I was staring at a gun aimed at my nose. He had managed to slide a gun inside my barely open car window. My life flashed before my eyes. I made a split second decision. I hit my electric power window button and trapped his hand and the gun inside my car.

"What do you want?"

"Give me your money!"

"I have no money."

"Roll down this window, or I kill you on the count of three."

5

≈

The Beginning of My End

"One... The word two... ricocheted through my brain. I realized I had only one precious second to live. In desperation, I reached for the gun with both hands and managed to rotate it toward my attacker. The gun was now on its side. I tried my best to shoot the SOB. My attacker was just as determined to save himself. He used his thumb to block the hammer.

At that moment, I realized I couldn't shoot him, and he could not shoot me. I floor boarded my gas pedal and away I went. When I looked in my rearview mirror, I saw him bend over to retrieve his gun. He somehow managed to pull his hand and the gun from my window's grip. Otherwise, my moving vehicle would have drug his butt along the long hot street.

My first thought. *I am going to turn around and run over the bastard.* My common sense objected. *No, stupid. He recovered his gun, and he plans to use it on you.* I raced my car to the first corner, turned left and left again. Two blocks later, I found two policemen in a golf cart vehicle writing a parking meter ticket. I sped toward the officers and stopped to tell them what just happened. Within minutes, they had a fingerprint unit on the scene to dust my blue Firebird for prints. Luckily, my attacker left a perfect palm print on the top of my car as he struggled to pull the weapon from my barely open car window.

After the fingerprinting ended, I lost it and broke down like a hysterical child. I could barely speak for my sobs. "I want to go home. I want to go home."

For three long months, I could not leave our house or go to work. I couldn't go anywhere. Bart drove me to the police station every time Detective Higgins called me to attend a lineup. Over the weeks, we saw more and more blonde victims came to the lineup room. I was one of only two women our attacker did not rape. Several girls reported that the creep tried to choke them unconscious before he raped them.

The Red Rock Rapist was the title in the local newspapers. He didn't want my money, he planned to rape me at gunpoint, had I not fought him and drove away. By the time he was arrested, he had raped ten blondes and two redheads. The last one was an illegal female from Mexico. Her attack proved to be the most savage. She was a virgin. He almost killed her. She never attended any lineups and disappeared from the city.

During this time, I approached Bart in our kitchen and surprised him with a request. "Take me to a gun range and show me how to fire your Magnum."

"Aren't you afraid of guns?"

"I am more afraid of having one used on me by some psycho."

He drove me to a local gun range several times a week for a month. My aim improved each time I fired his gun. I would envision the outline of The Red Rock Rapist on my paper target. One day, I finally reached my goal. All six bullets hit dead center on my target. *I just killed that son-of-a-bitch!* At least I did at the gun range.

The next time Detective Higgins called me in to view photos of possible suspects, I proudly showed him my paper target from the gun range. "We would have pinned a medal on you, if you had shot him that day. I wish you had turned your car around and flatten the creep."

"Believe me, I gave it strong consideration."

After three months, I knew it was time to return to work. Bart drove me downtown in his Blazer. "Wait for me. It won't take long to ask Mr. Gordon about returning to the parking lot."

Bart raised one eyebrow. "I'll be right here, doll."

Mr. Gordon was glad to see me, until I spoke. "I need back on the company parking lot. I never want to get mugged again."

"I can't help you. Only management parks there."

"Then I quit. My life is worth more than this job."

"After fourteen years, you would leave over a parking space?"

"That is exactly what I'm doing." I wheeled on my heels and left his office.

※ ※ ※

A year later, two female employees were mugged because they had to walk a long way and parked on the street. Ironically, one of them was Mr. Gordon's daughter. *Karma paid Mr. Gordon a visit.*

※ ※ ※

I climbed into Bart's Blazer after I left Mr. Gordon, and asked him to drive me to Adelle's workplace. I applied for a part-time job there. Through my mugging trauma, Bart was my rock.

Come Christmas morning he surprised me with a stunning red fox coat. As luck would have it, we came down with a bad case of flu that day. We opened presents and retreated to our sickbed.

Crystal ran errands for us with her new boyfriend, Eric Keys. He looked a lot like Elvis Presley. They dropped off some medicine for us, and they went to his house to avoid catching our flu. Stacy was still living with Tim and Dana.

About mid-afternoon, our frantic doorbell woke me up. I felt horrible, so I tried to ignore it, but the ringing persisted. I managed to walk to our door and open it. There stood Stephanie Kirby. She was Tim's live-in girlfriend.

"I need to talk to you."

"We're extremely sick with the flu. Please make it quick! I am too weak and feverish to stay up long!"

I managed to walk into the living room and eased onto my red Provincial chair. Stephanie sat on our white couch. "I'm sure you know that Tim and I have been seeing each other for over two years."

"Yes, and I do not like it, when my kids see the two of you sleeping together and you aren't married. My Mother taught me to never do that because it's wrong."

Stephanie ignored my remark. "I know the final hearing on Stacy's case is coming up in January. Something happened to me that you must hear before that hearing."

"Like what?"

"Tim hit me and knocked out my two front teeth."

"That's hard to believe. In five years of marriage, he never once threatened to hit me. He knew about the awful beatings I endured in my first marriage. I told him that I would do my best to kill any man who ever hurt me like that again. I find your news a bit hard to swallow."

"I'm here to tell you he did it! These front teeth are temporaries. My dental bill was well over a thousand dollars. Tim refused to pay for the damage he caused."

"Did you contact a lawyer?"

"Yes, and I filed assault charges with the police and put him under a Peace Bond."

"Peace Bonds don't work."

"There is more. When the officer served papers on Tim, he showed up drunk the same night and banged on my door. I called the police. Before they arrived, he relieved himself on the bushes and shouted obscenities at me. 'Whore, you'll pay for this!' He was three sheets in the wind, when the police arrived to arrest him."

"I am speechless. Thank you for telling me. I will call my lawyer tomorrow. He is about to take a sworn deposition from Tim. This will make a significant difference in the outcome."

After Stephanie left, I returned to my sickbed and told Bart what she had said.

I phoned Greg with the news. After the deposition, he called me with an update. "Tim turned white as a sheet, when I sprang questions on him about the Stephanie incident."

"That works for me."

✳ ✳ ✳

A week later, Detective Higgins phoned. "Debbie get down here for a lineup right now. We caught him."

"How can you be so sure?"

"The palm prints on your car nailed him."

"That makes me very happy!" Bart drove me downtown to the police station. He walked with me as far as they would let him go toward the line-up basement door. Detective Higgins led eleven of us down a winding staircase into the line-up room and took seats. He gave each of us a pencil and paper with numbers. "I want each of you to mark the number on your sheet that you believe is The Red Rock Rapist. I assure you, none of the suspects inside the line-up area can see you." He made a signal. The lights went off where we were sitting in the viewing room. Then the lights came on inside the line-up stage.

Each suspect had to speak certain words and then turn around slowly. I picked my choice as *The Red Rock Rapist* and marked my sheet. An officer told all the suspects to leave the line-up stage. Detective Higgins collected our papers. "Almost everyone picked out the same person. I know that we have a positive ID."

Before we left I approached him. "Who missed picking the right guy?"

"You did, but it is okay. Without his prints from your car, none of this would have happened tonight."

"Honestly, I could swear I picked the right creep. It all happened so fast for me that day. Plus, his gun was aimed at my nose and had my total attention."

✳ ✳ ✳

The following day, Tim's lawyer called Greg. He called to notify me that Tim dropped his child support claim, and he agreed to a more equitable settlement. January ended on a positive note. I enjoyed a few quiet days before another phone call came.

It was Detective Higgins. "The Red Rock Rapist case is on the docket for 10:00 a.m. on February 14th. Can you be there?"

"Yes, with bells on!"

"Great! Be there at 9:00 a.m. We need to prepare you for your testimony."

I suppose it was poetic justice that the trial date fell on *Valentine's Day, 1981.* I arrived at the Federal Courthouse, parked and took the elevator upstairs. Higgins introduced the three of us to Assistant DA Cline. The other two other ladies were raped by the monster. It was impossible for us not to be nervous about seeing our attacker face-to-face again.

Detective Higgins also brought in a female psychologist. She expected us to have strong emotions to deal with after we testified. She encouraged us to remain calm, when we first see him again, and try not to hold our breath. Detective Higgins and Assistant DA Cline prompted us with potential questions to hear our answers.

I can still see the rapist sitting at a table with his attorney. Why would a nice looking short Mexican with a round-face in his late twenties need to be a rapist? He had on a brown suit and tie. His mother and father were sitting behind him. As I testified, I noticed his beautiful young wife and their two lovely little girls sitting beside his parents.

Detective Higgins told us later, the rapist's father was a preacher, and he also built homes for a living.

In the end, the rapist's left handprint on the top of my car eventually caught him. Two undercover officers caught him as he made an illegal left turn one day and arrested him. When all our testimony was heard the jury conferred, and the Jury Foreman read the verdict. "Guilty as charged." The Red Rock Rapist received a prison sentence of twelve years. The verdict was a welcome relief for each of us. We never wanted to see his face again.

Higgins spoke to us before we left. "If anyone wants to write a letter and ask that this rapist serve more than twelve years because he is a danger to society, I will give them to the proper authorities."

We each wrote a letter with that request before we left that day.

✳ ✳ ✳

Later that night, Bart gave me a new dress from Frederick's of Hollywood and took me out for Valentine's Day supper. He drove us to a restaurant in his Blazer. During the evening, he gave me the eye and then said the strangest thing. "Doll, it makes no sense to be a goodlookin' woman like you and ever get married. If I were you, I would screw every man I could get my hands on."

His remark came out of left field and hit me cold. It left me confused and uncomfortable. Then he took a different route on the way home. He stopped at a small club I didn't know called, *Sansui*. He parked his Blazer. "Why are we stopping here?"

"I hear tell it's a relaxing place for a drink." He hopped out and hurriedly opened my door. As we entered the nightclub, a cold chill ran down my spine. The dark room had scant candle light in a few remote corners. Heavy cigarette smoke hung in the air. All the small round tables appeared occupied. I had trouble seeing the twenty couples sitting in the dim room.

Bart approached an attractive couple. "May we join you?"

A handsome man grinned. "Certainly."

I sat down and scooted close to Bart. He patted my knee. "Relax, doll."

I could hear a romantic song from the Fifties playing on a jukebox. The crowd looked to be in their mid-forties. Bart ordered us drinks from a skimpily dressed waitress. When she served our drinks, he tipped her generously and turned to me for a toast. "Here's to you, goodlookin'."

His head swiveled to scan the room and soak up the scenery. I wasn't sure whether to watch Bart or the intimate couples scattered around the room he was ogling. My mind began to spin. *What are we doing in this strange place? What is Bart thinking?*

Then I heard a familiar moan come from Bart. A smug smile covered his face as he squirmed in his seat. It angered me to realize the blonde next to him was rubbing her eager hand on his now-erect penis. *What does he think he's doing?*

My first impulse was to slap her, but Bart grabbed my hand first. "Relax, baby. This is a swinger's club. This goes on here all the time. They think nothing of it!"

During our conversation, the blonde kept fondling him and kissing his neck. I finally had enough and stood up. "Let's go!"

"Come on, sit down!" A sexy voice whispered from behind me. "Nothing happens here unless everyone agrees to it."

I turned to discover it was the blonde's attractive husband tugging on my hand for me to sit down, so I did. "Honey, is this your first time?"

"You could say that. It is also my last time."

"Do you know what a swinger's club does?"

"Not really."

"Couples swap partners sometimes. Look around this room. You will see couples mixing with other couples. The swapping happens elsewhere."

As I glanced at Bart. The blonde wife now had her hand down his pants. I tapped his shoulder. "Take me home right now!"

I cried all the way home. He remained silent, so I spoke. "Why did you take me to that place?"

"It was just curiosity thing."

✶ ✶ ✶

Life slowly returned to normal. My birthday was only weeks away. Inevitably, normal is short-lived in my current life. A week later, Crystal came home from her day at Red Rock High School and sat at our kitchen table. "Mom, some of my friends at school told me that Stacy's in a new play at a theater in our local mall called *Rocky Horror Picture Show*. I hear he is dressing up like a girl to portray Frankenfurter."

"Is it like a spoof on Halloween?"

"I'm not too sure."

The news about Stacy worried me. That weekend, I showed up at the mall, bought a ticket and went inside to see the play. It bowled me over to see Stacy prance onstage wearing heavy makeup, a curly black wig, a long black cape lined in red satin and very red high heels. As he sang a song, he dropped the black cape on the floor to reveal his skimpy Frankenfurter attire, complete with a form-fitting black corset and mesh hose. *You could have knocked me over with a feather.*

After the show I went backstage to see Stacy. It had been a long while. I missed him more than I could say. As I entered his dressing room, he stood up in full costume and makeup. "Mom, I want you to meet Patty North. She plays Magenta in the show."

I found Patty's personality adorable. She shook my hand and posed like Magenta.

She grinned. "I'm crazy about your son."

"So am I!" We both looked at Stacy. It was hard not to stare at his ultra-feminine costume. Even so, we visited for a while before the night ended.

✳ ✳ ✳

My birthday finally arrived. Bart took my hand as I made breakfast. "Baby, I want to take Crystal, Paulla, and you to a seafood restaurant tonight to celebrate your birthday."

"Is it seafood to die for?"

He grinned. "One can only hope."

Once we arrived, he was totally busy flirting with Crystal and Paulla that I felt like Cinderella without her glass slippers. He made Crystal the belle of my birthday ball the whole evening. *Once again, I feel non-existent. What is it with me and this invisibility thing and on my birthday no less?*

I am sure my face fell, when Bart turned to Crystal. "Kitten, you look good enough to eat!" She soaked up every moment of his adulation right in front of my face. I grew sicker and sicker at my stomach. *God help me disappear. I feel like I'm going to die.*

Bart talked around me the entire evening. He couldn't keep his hands off Crystal. He constantly stroked her hair, squeezed her arm or goosed her ribs. Granted, she's almost twenty, but I thought this was my birthday party?

The longer it went on, the more devastated I became. *Why is Crystal the center of Bart's attention tonight of all nights?*

Crystal's long blonde curls looked almost the same as the ones I had in high school. She is my daughter. He's my husband, and my so-called birthday party sucks.

When we arrived at home, I sat on our bed about to cry. Bart walked in and handed me a big pink box from Frederick's of Hollywood. I opened it and stared at two identical short nighties. I remember how pretty they were. Each one was a bright hot pink backless silk bodice, trimmed with a wide band of beige lace around the neck. I looked at Bart. "Why are there two of them?"

"I bought one for you, and one for Crystal."

"Her birthday is in December."

"She'll be twenty at the end of the year. I thought you would like my idea."

"I don't think so." I was perplexed. A sickening twinge of jealousy surged through the pit of my stomach. *Why is my husband showing my daughter all this attention tonight? And now this?* To put it bluntly, the whole evening made me feel like crap. *What is going on with Bart? I feel like I have been replaced by my daughter.* He left our room. I heard ripples of laughter from the hallway before they entered our bedroom all smiles.

He gazed at her. "Close your eyes, doll." He put her pink surprise from my box into her open hands. "Now you can look."

She squealed in glee. "How pretty. Is this for me?"

"Who else?" He winked at her.

The whole scene left me ill and speechless. It was such an in my face moment.

"Doll, why don't you and Crystal try them on for me? I want to take your picture together. You know like a mother and daughter moment."

It was all I could do not to explode. We changed clothes. Bart was ready with his Polaroid camera. I was totally uneasy over his requested photo session. *Whose idea could this have been? Surely not Crystals!* We stood side-by-side while Bart snapped photos of us with his Polaroid. "Now then, I want one picture with my 35mm camera." One ended up being four more.

Afterward, Crystal left and went to her bedroom. He closed our door, turned on the black light, shed his clothes and crawled onto our king-sized bed. *I thought we might finally have a tender night of lovemaking. Instead, I was in for yet another stunning surprise.*

"Doll, I want you to give me a little spanking tonight."

"What are you talking about?"

"I bought this today and I..." He leaned over his side of the bed and retrieved an object. Then he sounded like a little boy. "Whip me, Mommy. Show me that I was a bad boy." His eyes sparkled in anticipation as he placed a beige quirt into my nervous hand.

"I can't do that. I might hurt you!"

His voice grew breathless. "I want you to do it. It makes me excited just thinking about it!"

"I guess so, if you're sure."

He eagerly rolled onto his stomach. His body twitched with excitement. He waited and waited and waited. "Come on, kitten!" My heart was not in it. I drew the riding whip over my head and swung it toward Bart's nude body. I heard him sigh. "Oh my sweet kitten!"

✳ ✳ ✳

The word *kitten* transported me back to that awful day when I was four-years-old. Suddenly, I was reliving the terror of how my awful beating began. The echo of Mother's words brought me to tears. "Now your kittens will probably die because you bathed them."

When Daddy arrived, so did the snap of his belt. It sounded like a bullwhip. *My blue eyes filled with terror as my raging bull of a Daddy scolded me.* "I hear you bathed your kittens!" He kicked the rocking chair. I flew through the air and landed on my head. His gorilla-sized hands drug me outside. My heart pounded in fear. He yanked me into mid-air like a ragdoll and ferociously beat me with his belt. I went into *The Black Hole.*

As a four-year-old child, I was unable to realize the scope of the tragedy that had just unfolded. I was in extreme shock.

✳ ✳ ✳

Years later my psychotherapist, Betty T., told me it was abusive for a parent to set up a child for such life-threatening fear, not to mention the horrendous beating. *My kittens did not die. I was a helpless victim of child brutality.* That vicious beating might not have happened, if only Mother had paid attention to me when I turned on the bathtub water that day. That horrible beating by my dad ignited a stubborn streak in me to survive, in spite of the heavy odds.

I raised Bart's quirt and made an uncharacteristic remark. "I will get even with you for this, Daddy!"

Debbie's Parents

✳ ✳ ✳

"Yeah, I like that. Make me hurt!" Bart's comment snapped me back to reality.

I surveyed the scene before me. *How do I understand why Bart wants to thrust me into the role of an abuser? It makes my skin crawl. Did he commit some unthinkable deed to deserve such a beating?*

Given the events at my birthday party it fit my feelings about him. I gladly spanked him for the way he neglected me all evening to fawn over Crystal. *Is it my survival instinct kicking in from years ago? Maybe that explains my anger.*

Before the evening was over Bart persisted until I had delivered over two dozen blows to his exposed anatomy. He had a climax twice before I finished whipping him. My reward was that he spent an hour-and-a-half giving me a hot oil massage. *As I look back, it was a sad but sexually satisfying evening that left me in a state of total confusion.*

✳ ✳ ✳

I decided I wanted to attend a nearby Junior College to become a Realtor and sell real estate. A new direction in my life sounded inviting. Stacy rarely came by to visit because of Bart, and he only came when Bart was gone.

The following month, I received a phone call from Tim's mother, Dana. "Have you heard from Stacy?"

"No, isn't he in school today?"

"He is in some bad trouble."

"What happened?"

"He's somewhere in New Orleans. The police just called me. They are looking for him."

"Why is he in New Orleans?"

"He and several friends broke into Tim's rent house, stole lots of things, almost set the house on fire, drove to New Orleans and fell into some bad trouble there. Somehow, Stacy is the only one who managed to get away from the police."

"Good grief! I can let you know if he calls."

An hour later my phone rang. "Mrs. Austin?"

"Who is calling?"

"I am Officer Parker from the New Orleans Police Department. Have you heard from your son, Stacy?"

"No, I have not. How did you get my phone number?"

"One of his friends, named Donny, talked and gave us your phone number to get a lesser jail sentence."

"What did the boys do?"

"A lawyer from Atlanta, Georgia, lost his credit cards on Bourbon Street. The boys found them and charged their hotel room, food and other things on his cards, but the boys are lucky."

"How is that?"

"The lawyer had picked up a prostitute while he was in town. She stole his wallet and tossed the credit cards in the street where they found them. The lawyer is afraid to press charges because his wife will find out what he did."

"Thank Goodness!"

"American Express refuses to press charges unless the card holder agrees. The hotel fears bad publicity since the Mardi Gras is about to begin. They believe it isn't worth the business loss to file charges on the boys and receive bad publicity."

"Is everything settled?"

"No, Stacy's dad had to pay their huge hotel bill."

"Where are Stacy's friends now?"

"The Judge sentenced them to forty-five days in jail. Even though no one pressed charges, the State of Louisiana pressed them because they defrauded an innkeeper. Their crime is a misdemeanor here. We have an Arrest Warrant for your son."

"I told you, I haven't heard from him."

"Neither has his dad. He is flying to town tomorrow to drive your son's car back home. We told him we found a computer in the backseat. I was wondering if could be missing from your home."

"No. He is supposed to be living with his dad."

"If he contacts you, please call me."

"I certainly will." He rattled off his number and hung up.

Later, Bart phoned. "Doll, I have to work late tonight. A press broke down. I'm the only one who can fix it."

"I want to tell you about Stacy."

"It will have to wait. Here comes my boss. I must go."

I asked Crystal to phone Dan. She told her that she wired Stacy money for a bus ticket. He is on his way home. It amazed me that Tim allowed Stacy to return to his home after what had transpired.

✳ ✳ ✳

Days later, Bart came home with a gigantic whiskey bottle and put it in our living room. I followed him. "Did you buy that?"

"My boss gave it to me because I've worked so many hours."

"You aren't a drinker. What are you going to do with it?"

He shrugged. "I will think of something."

Bart's long hours grew worse. At first, I excused it since we needed the extra money. Six weeks passed. I decided to pull a page from the past and visit Bart at work.

Low and behold, a striking brunette named Gail greeted me as I entered. "Bart's at the airport with Rhonda to pick up a part."

"I'll wait." *I swear Miss Gail almost choked, when I sat down in Bart's office.*

6

≈

Humpty Dumpty Time

The moment Bart walked in and spotted me sitting in his office, he stomped to his desk and slammed a box of parts on it. "Why are you here?"

"I think we need to see more of each other. I came to take you out to eat the way we use to do."

Before he could respond, a soft high-pitched female voice interrupted. "Are you ready to go hon'?"

We looked up to see a shocked Rhonda at his door. The look on her face was priceless, when she saw me. I gave her the once-over. Her medium brown hair was in dog ears. She had tied them with blue ribbons just like *Daisy Mae.* She was almost wearing a white sleeveless blouse with a knot at her midriff and skimpy blue denim shorts. I have no idea how she squeezed into them. Her face appeared ordinary. Clearly, I was justifiably prejudiced.

I gave her one of my, "If looks could kill, you'd be dead" glares. It sent her scurrying from the room.

Bart jumped up and ran after her like a hound dog in heat. I could not believe my eyes.

Out of the blue, her dad, Cotton Marshall, approached me. "Can I get you something to drink? We have coffee and pop."

"No, thanks." I had no doubt that he knew exactly what was going on between them, and it made my blood boil.

Bart flitted in-and-out of his office several times without saying a word. I never budged. Determination kept me planted in that chair to wait him out. Finally, he stormed in the room and threw papers into his big brown briefcase and snapped. "Ready?"

"I sure am." I followed him outside. He climbed into his Blazer and glared at me from his perch behind the steering wheel. I walked to his passenger door, tapped the window and motioned for him to roll it down. "Where are we going?"

"Follow me. I'll show you."

My butt barely hit my car seat, when he slammed his Blazer into reverse. His rear tires squalled helplessly on the loose gravel. The top-heavy Blazer rocked side-to-side in a struggle to stay upright while moving. I could tell the night was shaping up to be a real humdinger. In three short blocks, Bart made a sudden right turn and parked in front of a bar, or should I say a dive. He exited the Blazer, strutted to the doorway of the *Green Glass Bar* and paused.

"Why are we here?" I questioned half-way out of my car.

"This is my Friday hangout where I drink with my friends." He scurried inside and left me in his dust. He knows I hate nightclubs and drinking because of my bad experiences with Harry and Tim. *I can't believe he expects me to go inside this dump and watch him get drunk.* Sadly, that is exactly what he did for the three long hours. It was difficult to sit there and watch the man I love openly flirt with every woman in the bar. I wasn't sure what he was trying to prove. Wisely, Rhonda and Gail never showed up.

All evening long, he continually mentioned another club across town. "Crystal should visit *Club Hero* near the airport and meet Rhonda and Gail. They all three like to shoot pool."

"I like to shoot pool, but no one in my family needs to hang out with any of your women friends."

"Maybe Crystal already has."

"Like hell."

Dear God, am I living in another universe? How did the man I love turn into such a big jerk? And we are nearing our eleven year anniversary.

By ten o'clock I stood up and tapped Bart's shoulder. "Give me your truck keys."

"Go home without me."

"I want your truck keys. I am driving you home right now. Let's go!" It was déjà vu. *One more time, here I am stuck in a smoke-filled bar telling another drunk it is time to go home. I already know his answer before he gives it.*

"Aw, honey. You know I love you."

Strange moods ebbed and flowed from Bart after that night. He was like a junkie in need of another fix. Cotton even gave him a raise to renovate his newly purchased warehouse, set up new stamping equipment and remodel his front offices.

✷ ✷ ✷

In the meantime, Crystal became severely ill and was unable to swallow. I spent days at a gastroenterologist's office while Dr. Sharp ran tests on her. When the multiple medical test results returned, he called for Crystal and me to visit his office.

"For some unexplainable reason, Crystal has developed a rare illness called Crohn's Disease."

"What would cause it? She has never mentioned any stress to me."

"It is caused from *extreme stress*." He turned to Crystal. "Do you feel overly stressed about anything, young lady?"

She shook her head. *"No, I don't."*

Her response surprised both of us.

"Mrs. Austin, there is no known cure for Crohn's Disease at this time. Her colon and small intestines have hundreds of ulcers. Should any of them penetrate her organ lining, she could die. Sometimes surgery is necessary to remove part of the small intestines. I am going to place her on a dangerous drug called *Prednisone.* The dosage must be increased slowly until her condition improves drastically. To remove her from the medicine too quickly would put her life at risk."

Shortly after going on Prednisone, Crystal began to crave salty pretzels. She would consume several bags of them every day. Her serious illness continued to mystify me.

One day, I approached Bart. "Why do you think Crystal has Crohn's Disease? Could she be doing too many school activities?"

"She is strong-willed just like you. It could be a genetic throw-back from her dad's side of the family."

"I could try to track him down and get his family's medical history."

"If that no good son-of-a-bitch, who broke your jaw, ever shows up here, I will probably kill him or make him wish I had. You'd best let that sleeping dog lie."

"I guess you're right. I don't need to talk to someone who tried to kill me eight times."

✳ ✳ ✳

That night, I dreamed about Stacy over-and-over. Each dream echoed the same message from him. "I love you Mom. I want to move home if Bart is gone." During the night, the sound of deep sobs awakened me. It surprised me to discover the sobs were mine. I grew more and more depressed each day. I was to the point where I'd wake up each morning and stare at the ceiling for over twenty minutes. It took every ounce of strength I could muster to drag myself out of bed. *My mind kept telling me odd things. Give up. Drive your car off a bridge. This sucking pain will never quit.*

The Committee inside my head showered me with even more depressing thoughts. *You're going insane. You might have a nervous breakdown. End it now.* In the end, my strong faith in God somehow kept me going through each painful day. The pain of depression felt like a giant metal claw had imbedded itself into the center of my chest. It took all of my strength just to breath. *Each morning, I wake up and dread being alive. I want to go back to sleep forever...*

✻ ✻ ✻

Years later, Betty explained to me that my depressed state was a scream for help. I needed a professional like her to survive.

✻ ✻ ✻

The day was *Monday, March 23, 1981.* It didn't feel any different from any other day. I finally rolled out of bed, in spite of that invisible clamp still clutched deep into my chest. Once again, it sucked almost every ounce of energy from my body. I stumbled into the living room, peered out our bay window and noticed that Bart had not driven his Blazer to work. Instead, he drove my old green Chevy that Mother gave me months earlier. It seemed odd. I finally dressed for work. It was my first week as a Realtor. I needed to take phone time. As I recall, nothing too memorable happened during that day. Later that night, Bart stayed out extremely late. Much later than usual. He never called, so I phoned Cotton at one a.m.

"Hi, this is Debbie Austin. Sorry to wake you. I am worried about Bart. He isn't home yet, and it's one o'clock."

"He went to Rhonda's birthday party with her brother Syd."

"I see. Thank you." I hung up. Another sick feeling slammed into the pit of my stomach. I paced the floor by our bay window. Finally, I reclined on our living room couch and dozed off. My chime clock from Mother rang twice and woke me up, just as a car door slammed out front. I walked to our bay window and watched Bart weave toward the front door. He fumbled with the lock and finally stumbled inside.

"Where have you been?" He pushed past me, trudged down the hall and passed out in our bed. Anger sent me after my pillow. I returned to the living room couch. Sleep was impossible. As I tossed and turned, the oddest thing happened. A soft male voice began to whisper in my left ear. It repeatedly insisted, *"Go. Look in the truck!"*

At first, I thought I must be hallucinating because I was the only one in the room, yet the voice persisted to whisper the same instruction over-and-over for over an hour. *Am I going mad?* I engaged in a mental argument with the voice. *Why should I look in Bart's truck? He drove my old green Chevy, not his Blazer Chalet.*

The voice finally won out because it refused to stop. It kept repeating, *"Go. Look in the truck!"*

I give up. What am I looking for? When no answer came, I eased into our bedroom to put on another warm gown, my red fox coat and warm house shoes. Finally, I snatched his keys from his dresser, found a flashlight in the kitchen and slipped out our front door. I was certain this was going to be a waste of my time. *What do you want from me, mystery voice? What is in Bart's Blazer?*

The nearby streetlight barely lit our front yard. I slid along our icy sidewalk and opened the passenger door. The dark interior seemed to growl at me. For over an hour, I dug through every nook, cranny, drawer, and closet inside the Blazer with the help of my flashlight, but found nothing. Finally, I stared at the last unopened drawer under a small bed to my left. I opened it and found myself surprised to see a huge white plastic bag. It was bulging with a white picture album, a large rolled-up poster, scads of 8x10 photos stuffed into a manila envelope and a cigar box with *Crystal printed on the top by a pencil.*

I carried the heavy bag to the front seat and sat in the passenger seat. I pulled out the photo album, readied my flashlight and opened the album cover to look at the first page. *It feels like an atomic bomb just went off inside of me, and I am no more!*

Bart's Blazer Chalet

7

≈

Journey of Anguish

To this day, *I believe God sent that whispering angel to convince me to, Go! Look in the truck! It was no fluke.* God intervened in my life at that exact moment for a reason. He wanted me to see something in that blasted Blazer, so I gripped my flashlight in one hand and shined the light on the first album page. My heart sank. Pictures of nude women I had never seen before sucked the breath from my body. Later pages revealed women I did know like dear old Beulah, baseball scorekeeper Marty, Bart's ex-wife Joan, his co-worker Gail, and, of course, *dearest Rhonda.*

Each photo delivered a harsh blow to my heart. I saw women in motel beds and others in homes I'd never seen. I grew sicker with the turn of each new page. All feeling vanished from my numb body. The freezing temperature of that March morning couldn't faze me. My anger surfaced from a deep place only to run and hide. I was saturated with waves of unbelievable betrayal. *The more pages I view, the more I feel like the remains of Hiroshima.* My world just exploded into a billion pieces of shrapnel. Halfway through the thick album, I slowly turned the page. *Did a shotgun blast just blow my head off?* I was staring at a young photo of Crystal. She was about ten-years-old. She was standing in our living room with straggly hair, braces, no bra, just panties.

Somehow, I forced myself turn each page in the last half of that huge picture album. I saw the most disgusting sexually explicit pictures of my daughter all the way to the current time.

I sat there trembling in shock and disbelief over my sickening discovery. *Life just ended for me. Strangely, my body forgot to die. My mind shut down. I could barely breathe. It seems like I am having an Out-of-Body Experience from Hell.* I unfolded a paper from one of the last few album pages and stared at it. It contained a handwritten poem that Bart addressed to me. Ironically, he wrote it on my birthday eleven days earlier. It was the same day he ignored me to flirt with Crystal and Paulla, and then later, he wanted me to spank him with his new quirt. *Too bad I didn't destroy his ass with that quirt!*

3-12-81

"To Debbie:

Eulogy for a Love Affair

Yesterday night, making love with you was the same to me as brushing my teeth.

I felt better afterwards, but it was routinely done with robot precision.

And all the decision and anticipation gone, brushed away with over-familiarity.

This morning, when you kissed me good-bye, there was no chill inside of me.

I know how you kiss, and your secret ways are not secret to me anymore.

And all the curiosity and expectation gone. Kissed away with over-informality. I can't let go. Can you?

I hold on to what is gone and know my fingers grasp nothingness and tighten my already clenching grip.

I don't want to have to learn it all again with someone new, but there is no feeling in me when I see you.

I am dead-weight under your roving touch that knows all the places and spaces.

I am bored to tears, which you mistake for my pleasure.

I will never stop loving you as I have never stopped loving those who came before you.

Anticipation and new expectations are my lifeblood.

Forgive me for knowing you too well, or perhaps it is that you know me.

And I do not wish to be known."

✻ ✻ ✻

Eons of time swept before my lifeless eyes, after I read his aptly titled poem. I tried to focus and resume my *Journey of Anguish* through Bart's remaining keepsakes. I placed the Tampa Nugget cigar box with Crystal's name printed on the top in big letters and clearly written by her, on my lap. Inside, I found a stack of handwritten letters to Bart from her. Many were dated as far back as four years ago. I read each story and sank even further into a dark hole buried somewhere deep inside the remains of my broken soul. Each word like deep stab wounds to my heart. Every story was of her creation. Things she wanted to read to Bart when they were alone. Each one was rife with *BDSM acts* she planned to perform on him the next time they were alone.

✻ ✻ ✻

Looking back today, Crystal's stories might even give *50 Shades of Gray* a run for its money.

✻ ✻ ✻

My pounding heart felt like a sledge hammer that was pounding nails into the coffin of my life as I once knew it. Then another wave of pain hit me like an electrical shockwave. I pulled out Bart's large manila envelope with a stack of 8x10 black-and-white photos inside. I discovered they were all of the same nude picture of my daughter. *God, please tell me Bart isn't selling Crystal's pictures to someone.*

Last of all, I unrolled the huge poster sticking out of the bag. It was also in black-and-white. I stared at it for the longest time. It was of my nude daughter lying prone across the bed I thought I only shared with my husband, Bart... *Just shoot me!*

I slowly put everything back into the plastic bag and wrapped the bag tenderly with my numb arms. *I held it close to my heart as if it was a newborn child that had just died. I rocked it back-and-forth in the cold darkness for what seemed an eternity. It was symbolic of the death of my life, my love, my marriage and possibly of me.*

Various emotions poured through my mind like a volcano spewing red-hot lava in all directions. Helplessness prevailed in places I had never felt before. *It is as if someone just shot me, but for an unknown reason my body continues to move.*

How could I have not known? Why didn't Crystal tell me? Despair stomped on my broken heart. Betrayal swam through my veins. Anger ravaged my soul. Bart does not deserve to live another hour. I gritted my teeth. *Extreme shame shattered the remnants of my now fragile self-esteem.* I gave Bart and my kids one-hundred percent of me, and I saved nothing for myself. Unbearable pain punctured my every pore. No words known to man could describe the pain and despair that tortured every cell of my being. *Every minute corner of my body feels flattened. All fear strangely vanished. I have nothing to live for. What more can I lose now besides my life?* I was dangerously close to empty. My world had just exploded. *Why in the hell am I still breathing?*

Yet, I knew I must return one last time into my home and confront Bart. Then, I slid his truck key into the ignition and started the engine. I half expected to see him storm out our front door any moment because he would think someone was stealing his precious monster. Hurriedly, I stomped the gas pedal. The Blazer slid part way to the nearest corner.

I had no idea where I was going or what I was going to do with all the pictures, letters and poster I had just found in that white satchel. All I knew was, I must hide them in a safe place from Bart.

At the end of the street, I wheeled right and then left, ran a stop sign, barely made another left at the next corner and ran a second stop sign. I almost rolled the top-heavy Blazer while making a right turn on the icy street. *God must have sent an Angel to get behind the wheel of Bart's Blazer that morning. Otherwise, it would have rolled over and killed me instantly.*

The cold dark streets appeared eerily deserted on that now *infamous Tuesday morning.* I drove south and checked the side mirrors. I still half expected to see Bart following me at any moment in my blue Firebird. With no destination in mind, I continued down the lonely street going who knows where. I unexpectedly whipped a right and drove down Adelle's street. *It was as if God's Hand grabbed the steering wheel and turned it right.*

The Blazer came to a sliding stop in front of Adelle's small brick home. Two huge trees hung over the west side of her yard. A nearby streetlight cast an eerie ghost-like shadow onto the face of her home. In the dimness of the morning, I vaguely recall stepping from the Blazer while clutching that white satchel. I approached her door and punched the doorbell.

The extreme chill of the morning air failed to faze me. I rang her doorbell again, until her porch light lit up. Adelle's Southern drawl called out from behind her door. "Debbie, is that you?"

"Help me!" A soft child-like voice cried out from somewhere inside my almost lifeless body. She opened her door.

"It's 4:30 in the morning. Are you hurt? Please come inside."

Without saying a word, I walked past her and entered her kitchen. *I continued to cradle the white satchel I was holding as the remnants of my destroyed life.* I felt as if I had been, "Rode hard and put up wet," as Bart liked say.

I sat on Adelle's straight-back kitchen chair. *I hugged the white satchel with both arms for dear life and rocked it non-stop.*

She brushed her brown hair out of her eyes, sat in a chair across the kitchen and stared at me. She was nine-years-older than me. Our friendship had endured several disagreements through the years. Even so, we remained friends. She finally spoke. "Can you tell me what happened?"

I shook my head from side-to-side in deathly silence.

She stood up and made herself a cup of coffee. "Would you like a Diet Coke?"

My head rolled in more silence.

She carried her cup of coffee to a chair. "Honey, I can't help you if I don't know what is wrong."

I gazed at her with unblinking eyes. I was unable to talk or cry. *Unbelievable shock has me firmly locked in its wicked grip.*

"Can I see what you have inside your satchel?"

My head dropped backward and then forward. The word never managed to roll off my lips. It echoed through her yellow kitchen.

"Honey, tell me what happened. You have to..."

My eyes were fixed on a spot on her floor about four feet to my left. I took a long deep breath and closed my eyes. *Finally, a bitter sigh shot forth from me. It sounded more like a death moan.* "Oh Adelle. I don't know what to do."

"Please tell me what is in the satchel. I know it must be bad. Will you tell me anyway?"

"It's Bart... I found them hidden in his Blazer. A strange voice kept telling me, 'Go! Look in the truck!' Finally, I did... *They're awful, Adelle, just awful.*"

"I know you are right, but what are they?"

"No one can see them. Help me hide them. Bart can never know where they are. They are my only evidence."

"Why do you need evidence?"

"I just do, and I must go home and confront him."

"Why not stay here with me?"

"I can't! Crystal is still there asleep."

"You should be scared of Bart. Everyone knows how dangerous he is."

"I'm not afraid of him."

"So tell me, are there photos in that satchel?"

"I will let you see two of them that I'm taking home, you must promise not to look at the rest of them. Promise me you will only hide them. Promise me. Please!"

"I promise. Now, I want you to go to the police instead."

"No. I'm going home and wake up that drunken son-of-a-bitch and confront him! *I want to know. I have to know, why?*"

"Honey, please stay here! I am afraid he will kill you. *He will be like a trapped animal.*"

"Yes, but I will have this satchel hidden. He is going to demand it all back. It's my ace-in-the-hole. You will have it."

"Let me see the images you are keeping out. I can hide his satchel in my attic. He can't find them, even if he comes here."

I carefully removed two eight-by-tens from Bart's big family album and showed them to Adelle. She gasped and grabbed her heart when she saw them. "Oh honey, I am sorry you are in this much pain. *My heart hurts for you." She broke down and cried so hard that she had to cover her face with both hands.*

"From what I can tell, Bart made so many duplicates that he must have been selling her pictures to someone." I stood up and slowly moved toward her front door. She grabbed me in a moving trembling hug. Non-stop tears rolled down her reddened cheeks. My shock-filled body remained incapable of shedding tears or saying another word. I felt like a numb zombie as I left her standing at her door crying on that cold March morning.

Frankly, I doubt my ability to ever feel normal again, much less be able to cry...

8

≈

Time to Confront the Devil

I stepped into Bart's now-memorable Blazer and drove home. I did not rehearse or plan my speech. It was rare for my mind to remain totally still. It felt as if the eye of a hurricane waited deep inside of me to explode in a fury at any moment.

Once I was home, I parked the Blazer where it was earlier when I prowled through it. I opened the Blazer door, picked up the two heart-wrenching photos and walked inside our house.

In the hallway things turned hazy. I barely recall entering our bedroom to confront Bart. *The bastard needs to be shot, like the animal he is, for doing this to my daughter.*

I found him still sprawled out in our king-sized bed snoring from his heavy consumption of alcohol. I placed both pictures on the foot of the bed and turned on the bright spotlight above our headboard. The light hit him in the face. He stirred briefly and threw the covers over his head.

I punched his shoulder extra hard. "Tell me about these pictures!"

"Huh? What the fuck do you want?" He mumbled from under the sheet and then rolled to the center of the bed.

"Tell me about these pictures!"

"Go to Hell, bitch!" He flipped the overhead light off and disappeared under the covers again.

I walked to his chest of drawers, opened the top drawer, grabbed his loaded .357 Magnum and turned toward the bed. Vaguely, I recall shouting at Bart. *"Time for your ass to go to Hell, Mother Fucker!"* Six rapid shots rang out. His blood splattered our bedroom. The reality of what I had just done was unclear to me. Blood dripped from our formerly lacy white curtains hanging around our now blood-soaked bed. I stared at our bloody mirrored headboard and saw a motionless female holding a Magnum.

Crystal raced into the room in her pajamas and screamed at me. *"Why did you shoot him? Don't die Bart! I love you!"*

✳ ✳ ✳

Months later, Bart's attorney told me in private, "No jury would have ever convicted you for killing him, after what you found in that pornographic satchel of his. He is one lucky man that you didn't blow him away that morning."

✳ ✳ ✳

Truthfully I never once considered shooting Bart that morning. Adelle told me that if that had been her finding those awful satchel contents, Bart would not have known what hit him."

✳ ✳ ✳

I did enter our bedroom, and I found him still sprawled out on the bed snoring and still drunk from Rhonda's birthday party. I flipped the bright spotlight on. It hit him in the face, as I placed both pictures on the foot of the bed. He barely stirred before he threw the covers over his head.

I punched his shoulder hard. "Tell me about these photos!"

"Don't fuck with me bitch!" He mumbled from under a sheet and then rolled to the center of the bed.

"Tell me about these damned pictures now!"

"What are you talking about?" He half-shouted in disgust and slowly sat up with an ugly scowl.

"Those two right there on the foot of the bed!" I pointed at the large pictures.

He leaned forward, saw them, stepped out of bed and looked me square in the eye. "Where are the rest of them?"

"Safely hidden. You will never find them. If anything happens to me, the police will get them. Now tell me why you did this to Crystal!"

Bart stood up, pushed past me, opened his closet and pulled the string to turn on his closet light.

I pivoted toward his now bent-over frame inside the closet. "Explain those pictures to me, damn it!"

No response. He turned and glared at me. I watched him step into his tight jeans, fling on a plaid shirt, slip on socks, step into his cowboy boots, zip his jeans and put on his western belt. "Well?" I persisted.

His hazel eyes shot holes through me. They were filled with hateful nothingness. He returned to his closet to gather his guns. I knew he had a Magnum and an antique gun, but I had no idea he had a small arsenal in there. He carefully wrapped each weapon in a hand towel, packed them inside his old brown suitcase, picked it up and walked out of our bedroom. I heard the front door open.

I wasn't sure what to expect from him. I stared into his open closet. Minutes passed before I heard the ever-familiar sound of his boots crisply strutting down the hallway. That no longer brought joy to my heart. *I feel like one of the Living Dead.*

Bart hurried into his closet and resumed gathering his things. He carried several loads of clothes to his Blazer and then emptied the rest of his closet. Then he packed his shaving kit and colognes from the master bathroom into a small brown zipper bag and walked toward our bedroom door like a mechanical robot.

I dogged his steps. "I want the Magnum." He pulled it from his belt, unloaded it and placed it on the bed. Then he added his antique gun from his boot and stormed out the front door.

The life I cherished just disintegrated before my eyes. *God's Whispering Angel* accomplished his goal and returned to the heavens. I was left to run on empty. I wanted to die! A haze surrounded me as I followed Bart in a state of shock. My eleven year marriage to the man of my dreams had vanished into *The Winds of Why.*

He paused at the front door. "I will call when I'm ready for my other things." An icy coldness ran after him as he drove away.

I stood at our front door in deepening shock. Is this bottomless emptiness all that remains of my life? My world just disappeared in a puff of smoke. I just want to die. Crystal slept through our altercation. I closed the front door and shut my eyes.

✳ ✳ ✳

Our airplane suddenly shook because of a bad thunderstorm and startled me. Slowly, I closed the book. Tears welled up in my eyes for this poor woman and her heart wrenching experience. *God, how can she ever exist after this? Or can she?*

The stewardess sat in the empty seat beside me. She sniffled and pounded her fists on the armrests. "If Bart had been my husband, I would have blown the scumbag to pieces."

I nodded, took a deep breath and reopened my book to resume following the unfolding tragedy...

✳ ✳ ✳

As I walked into our formal living room, I realized those two awful pictures were dangling from my hand. I tried not to look at them, yet I sat down and stared at them for the longest time. An hour passed. Crystal woke up and found me in the living room. I was hugging the two photos, listening to country music and had entered an unseen world to survey the ruins of my life from another harbor. It was somewhere inside of a vast black hole.

"Mom, since when do you listen to country music?"

My eyes slowly rolled toward her and then looked the other way. An eerie stillness filled the room. I must have scared her.

"What's wrong, Mom?"

Without looking her way, I whispered. "Bart's gone."

"Gone where?"

"He is gone for good."

"What do you mean?"

"I mean we are getting a divorce!"

"Why?"

"I know about the two of you." I forced my eyes to meet her green eyes. *"Why in God's name didn't you tell me? I don't understand that. I'll never understand why you didn't let me know."*

She sat on our deep red carpet near my chair and looked up at me. "I was afraid of Bart. I didn't think you would believe me."

"Why wouldn't I believe you? You're my daughter."

"Bart scared me. That's all I know."

"Surely, you could have told me, Paulla, someone, anyone."

Silence settled over the room. Endless questions ricocheted through my mind. *How do I move forward from this point? How can I tell my family about the atrocity that just surfaced from the Depths of Hell, without feeling ashamed of not knowing or not seeing that a Snake Charmer fooled me for eleven years? Can I survive this unbearable pain? Who is going to be there to help me survive? Can I survive?*

I revisited the two pictures I was clutching against my chest. *God, I feel so betrayed. How do I ever trust Crystal after reading all of those decadent stories she wrote to Bart about the erotic BDSM sex she planned to do with him? How do I know she didn't like what I saw in those sickening photos? Her stories show no indication of fear.* One picture that Bart took of her showed her standing in our bedroom wrapped in my new red fox coat that he recently gave me for my Christmas present. It was draped over her bare shoulders and nude body. Another one was a raunchy porn-like shot of her posing nude on our pool table with her legs spread-eagle while she used a dildo on herself.

There was only one shot of Bart. Crystal took it while standing up. It was of him on his knees giving her oral sex. My mind kept returning to her handwritten sex stories. They were full of raunchy adult sex and lots of bondage she wanted to do with my husband in our bed, on our pool table, in our swimming pool, in the toolshed, his Blazer and God knows where else. I have no doubt that Crystal wrote all of them. I know my daughter's handwriting.

What a dumbass I've been. I gave everything I had to Bart and my kids. What happens to me now? How can I ever trust anyone again? *I feel as if someone shot a huge hole through my chest, and my body refuses to die. How can God do this to me? The pain is unbearable! Hell, I can't even weep for myself. My tears ran and hid somewhere in the depths of my shattered soul, afraid to share in my grief. Why am I living this hellish nightmare? I am sinking with from an anchor of disbelief. Inside, I am lonely, deserted, hurt, ruptured and deathly empty.*

It was impossible for me to function. I managed to stand up. I walked to my bedroom, shut the door and sat on my bed. *I stared into nothingness for hours.* I don't know what Crystal did after I left.

Sleep escaped me all night. My eyes refused to close. *I feared more atrocities would move in from another hidden source and attack my wavering sanity.* I sat propped up in bed all night and found myself fighting to exist in the vacuum I once called my soul. The light on my white French provincial desk by my bed allowed me to observe my bedroom. *It seemed I could somehow see the scene of a senseless murder where a child mutilation had occurred. Yet, I am the one who feels mutilated, inside and out. I shut down and ceased to function. I have no appetite, sleep, concentration, tears, anger, emotions, and no me. Am I going mad? God, please take me right now!*

On Wednesday, I drove to my real estate office to take phone time and keep my mind occupied. Mrs. Janski, now my Office Manager and formerly from Little Ones, could tell by looking at me that something was horribly wrong. She approached and tenderly placed her arm on my shoulder, as I sat at my desk and stared out the window. "I don't know what is wrong, Debbie, but I'm here if you want to talk."

I bit my lip. I was unable to respond. I nodded in the affirmative and glanced at her briefly. I didn't want her to look into my eyes. I feared she might be able to see the horror I had just lived through the past twenty-four hours.

✻ ✻ ✻

Each day and night grew longer than the last one. *Sleep is impossible. I desire no food. I exist on a strange form of adrenaline I never felt before.*

By Thursday, I agreed to work a night hire where Adelle and Lori worked. The minute I entered the side door of the one-story building, Adelle saw me through the cafeteria glass window. She bolted through a doorway and met me in the hall. "I'm so glad to see you."

"Why? Did something happen?"

"Do you think Bart suspects I have those pictures?"

"No. Why?"

"I saw him drive by my house many times last night."

"There is no way he could guess where I hid the evidence. He hasn't called. I have no idea where he is staying. I'll call his work and ask his friend, Justine Bradley." I hurried to the employee phone in the cafeteria and dialed her work number.

"Justine, do you know what happened between Bart and me?"

"I know some of it."

"Do you know where Bart is staying?"

"He's at Rhonda's apartment."

"Doesn't she have two young children?"

"Yes, a boy five and a girl nine."

I hung up the phone and prayed. *Please God, Bart must never have any more children within his grasp. He can't be allowed to stay with Rhonda's kids.*

Come morning, I phoned Justine again and managed to get Rhonda's address from her. Before I could drive to her apartment, one of my worst migraine headaches struck with a vengeance. I swallowed two migraine pills, and because I had eaten very little in over a week, I became extremely sick and went to bed. The severe pain almost knocked me out cold.

When Crystal came home from school that afternoon, she tried to rouse me with little success. She grew frantic and phoned

Mother. "Please come quick! There is trouble here. Bart moved out. Mom is in bed asleep with a migraine. She hasn't eaten in almost a week. I can't wake her up. Please, come help us!"

I slept through the night. I finally managed to get up at 8:00 a.m. I vaguely recall driving to my Saturday morning accounting class at a nearby junior college. My mind was in a fog from the shock of the past week, a head-splitting migraine and only a few hours of forced sleep.

As I arrived in class, I eased into a desk seat at the back of the room. Our instructor began to ask questions of random students. I prayed he'd skip me because I knew I couldn't answer think. It was hard to even focus on my notebook to take notes. Unexpectedly, *I began to hyperventilate. My breathing was intermittent. I gasped for air. Frustration smothered me like a giant web. I grabbed my books and fled.* Somehow, I managed to find my car on the sprawling parking lot where I left it minutes earlier.

For an unknown reason, I drove past my home. Crystal's car hadn't moved. I topped the hill doing forty miles-an-hour. Within in twelve blocks, I turned into the apartment complex where Rhonda and her children lived. At the third row of buildings, I spotted his Blazer. Rhonda's baby blue pickup was right beside it. With zero fear, I marched to several apartment doors and knocked. "Do you know Rhonda Marshall? She lives in these apartments."

"Never heard of her." That was the standard reply.

I glanced around and spotted a young boy and a girl playing with toy trucks underneath a see-through cement stairway to the second floor. "Do you know where I can find Rhonda Marshall?"

"Sure do. That's our mom." The tow-headed boy replied.

"Would you show me your apartment door?"

"Okay." He jumped up and led me up the stairs. His blonde-headed sister followed us up the turning stairway. He pushed their unlocked door open. "Mom, you have company."

Her high pitched voice replied. "Tell them to have a seat."

I followed the youngsters inside their apartment. They hurriedly disappeared into their room. The messy apartment and poor furnishings surprised me, since her daddy owned a big company. It reminded me of what I would call *Early Garage Sale Era*. I scoped out the room for any sign of Bart with no luck. A tattered brown chair appeared in the best shape, so I sat down.

Rhonda's tall thin figure flowed into the room wearing a black silk robe. Big pink foam rollers covered her light brown hair. Inadequate make-up failed to hide her ordinary face. I could not imagine Bart wanting anyone who stood two inches taller than him. He's extremely self-conscious about his height and has a serious Napoleon Complex.

"Rhonda, I want to talk to you about Bart!"

"There is nothing you can tell me that I want to hear!"

"It's about your kids and..."

Bart entered the room in a bathrobe, sat on her dingy brown couch and glared at me.

"Why are you here?"

"I came to warn her about what you will do to her kids."

Rhonda served Bart a hot cup of coffee. "There is nothing I want to hear from you about Bart." She returned to her small kitchen to get herself a cup of coffee and quickly sat beside him. "Unless it comes from Bart, I'm not interested in anything you have to say!"

"It concerns your children!"

"What about them?"

"Do you want him to do this to your young daughter?" *I handed her a picture of Crystal that I found in Bart's Blazer that morning. The photo was the one of her at age ten. She was standing nude in our formal living room with straggly hair, braces and a yet-to-be-developed young body.*

For a moment, I thought the photo had reached Rhonda because she stared at it intently. The Snake Charmer had other plans. I watched him slide his arm around her shoulder and tenderly stroke her cheek. In seconds, he had pushed all of her buttons and was instantly in control of her logic. *It's amazing how fast he worked her.*

"That means nothing to me. It will never happen to my kids." She stood up and left the room. I noticed she left Crystal's photo on their coffee table.

It was hard to look into Bart's hate-filled eyes. I found it even harder to accept how fast he swooped into Rhonda's life with an instant family. It was as if he had merely changed clothes.

"Go home Debbie." His defiant eyes drilled holes thru me.

Suddenly, a loud noise came from Rhonda's hallway. I whipped my head toward the direction of the sound. *Rhonda pumped her shotgun and looked at Bart. "If that ever happened to my daughter, I wouldn't file for divorce. I would kill the son-of-a-bitch in his sleep."* She raised her shotgun high for emphasis. "I can take care of my kids. Now, why don't you leave?"

I reached for Crystal's picture. Bart's hand also raced for it. "There will be no more photos of my daughter for you!"

I stood up and left the small apartment with Crystal's photo in hand. As I sped away, I felt I had failed Rhonda's children. They are in tremendous danger, and Rhonda totally ignored my plea.

My Firebird topped the slight hill close to home. I saw Mother's black Impala parked out front.

✹ ✹ ✹

I don't need this right now! I parked my car and wandered inside. *Disappointment trailed behind me like an invisible monster.*

"Momma, what are you doing here?"

"Crystal called me. She's worried about you. What happened?"

I cut her short. "I can't talk about it!" I fled to my bedroom and slammed the door. My raw feelings were too fresh for discussion, especially with Mother.

Late that evening, she entered my bedroom. "I don't know what happened. Your face tells me it must be awful. Can you tell me what happened?"

"No."

"Honey, you cannot go on like this. You look terrible. Maybe you need to see a doctor."

"Maybe I do." I reached for my black portable radio. Momma realized I wasn't going to talk, so she left my room. I shut my door, sat on the bed and found a country song on the radio. I had always hated country music because of that awful nasal twang. Suddenly, I could relate to the sad lyrics woven into those songs.

One tune in particular reached out and grabbed my aching heart. It was the moving words from Alabama's new hit tune, "Old Flame." *The words in that song scorched my broken heart like a branding iron. Finally, my tears began to flow as if a monsoon had been released.*

During the coming weeks, I struggled to keep myself afloat in a dark sea of devastating depression. I could not stop crying. Black moods smothered me. Withdrawal and a chest pain, I can't describe, pulled me lower and lower into a more depressed state. I resented breathing and grew dangerously hopeless.

A turning point came the following Monday. I took too many aspirin for my depression. Mother demanded I see a doctor to get some anti-depressants. She and Crystal helped me to her car and drove me to a doctor. Afterward, she picked up my prescription and insisted I take one of the pills in her car.

We were almost home. My head felt as if it had vanished from my shoulders, but my tears were subsiding. Within a block of the house, I looked up and saw Bart cruising toward us in his Blazer.

"I guess he wanted to revisit the scene of his crime, no doubt!" When we passed him in the middle of the block, he looked at me with the eyes of a total stranger. I wondered what he wanted just as the pills made me too relaxed to give a damn.

For the first time in weeks, I slept through the night. The medicine knocked me out. When morning came, my phone woke me up. Archie Raines, my boss where I now worked part-time, wanted me to work that night. I found Archie attractive, in his mid-fifties, an ex-Marine with mostly white hair and a reputation for being quite a rounder. Years ago, he had a scuffle at a Union Meeting and bit a chunk out of his antagonist's ear.

I could heard his voice through the phone. "Gal, I need to hire you for tomorrow night. Can you make it?"

"I guess."

I managed to drive to work that afternoon. For a while I actually functioned, until the pills wore off and my tears returned with a vengeance. They blinded my vision and flooded my mind with horrible memories. I swallowed two more anti-depressants and ran to the restroom to fix my smeared make-up.

Charlotte Sassy Hall was a small thin woman in her fifties and a rabid smoker with a permanent scowl. She entered the restroom and glared at me through her glasses. "What's wrong with you?"

I barely acknowledged that rude person.

"I had a fight with my husband last night, but I'm too strong to let a man get me down." She turned and left.

Thirty minutes later, I returned to work only to rush back to the restroom and cry my eyes out again. I replaced my make-up for a second time and took another anti-depressant. I forgot I hadn't eaten in days. My tongue swelled up so big that I was unable to say a coherent word. Adelle and Lori found me in a chair unable to move or talk. My swirling head made me nauseous. Lori ran to call my doctor. Adelle phoned Crystal.

Mother and Crystal arrived in fifteen minutes. Several people had to help me into Mother's car. Crystal drove my car home. On the way, Momma put her foot down. "I want to know what's going on. You are killing yourself. What in the world did Bart do to you?"

My swollen tongue made it almost impossible to breathe much less talk. Mother and Crystal helped me in our house and to my bed. *I had a strange thought before I dozed off. Maybe Bart hopes I'll die. Then, he will be off the hook.* That idea generated a tiny spark of determination in me to live. It flickered somewhere deep inside me.

✷ ✷ ✷

I once read, "When you get to the end of your rope, tie a knot and hang on." That is what I did that night. I tied a knot and hung on until morning. When I woke up I felt somewhat normal, until that black depression tornado swept toward me again and implanted itself deep into my chest. I phoned Adelle at work.

"Is there a Hotline number I can call? I need help."

"Call 1-888-444-HELP and tell them what happened. They will find you a doctor to help you."

Quickly, I sat on the bed and dialed the number. A kind lady answered, heard my story and made an emergency appointment for me at Stoneway Medical Center in two hours.

I said a prayer. Thank you, God. I hope this works. Maybe someone can help me deal with my horrific depression, heartbreak and shattered life. All I want is for the pain to stop. It is pulling me further and further down a dark hole to certain death.

Vaguely, I recall what the young psychiatrist looked like. It took me thirty minutes to explain to him what I had been through. As I revisited the events, my depression increased. My inability to come to grips with Bart and Crystal's possible love affair took a nosedive. I could feel my will to live collapsing all around me. He was my last hope.

He cocked his head, leaned back in his chair and smugly made an assessment. "From what I heard, you do not have a problem."

Clearly, he can't be serious? "What do you mean, I don't have a problem?"

"As far as I can tell, you're fine."

Rage shot through me like a bolt of lightning. I wanted to climb over his desk and choke him. Instead, I jumped to my feet. *"If I don't have a problem, I'll just go shoot the son-of-a-bitch. Then you'll be right. My fucking problem will be dead!"* I stormed out of his office. That was the first time in my life I had ever used the "F" word.

On the way home, I drove like a crazed maniac powered by consuming outrage. That moment turned me on a dime. My tears ceased. I instantly decided to do whatever it takes to see that Bart pays dearly for what he has done to me and my children.

At home, I rushed to my bedroom, shut the door and phoned my attorney. "Greg, I want to file divorce papers today. Call me when the papers are ready, and I'll come sign them."

✳ ✳ ✳

The time had finally come to tell Momma what Bart had done to Crystal. I sent Crystal on an errand to the grocery store. After she left it was time. I sat at my kitchen table and looked at Momma on the den couch. "Come over here, and I will me tell you what's wrong with me."

A worried look covered her face. She carried her cup of coffee to the table and sat across from me. "Okay, let's have it!"

"I do not know an easy or gentle way to say this, but here goes. In the early hours of March 23rd, a strange invisible voice of an Angel whispered to me for one hour. 'Go! Look in the truck!' When I did I found a big white satchel filled with a bulging white photo album, reprints of 8x10's, a large poster and a cigar box with a huge stack of handwritten pornographic stories that Crystal wrote to Bart while she was in school. Most of the images inside that white album were of her. He took the youngest photo of her shortly after we married. He's been sexually abusing her and..."

Momma's palm shot toward me. "Stop! I can't hear any more of it." She looked as if I had knocked the breath out of her. For several minutes, she drifted into private thoughts and eventually resurfaced. "Why didn't Crystal tell you?"

"Dear God, I wish I knew. She claimed he frightened her."

"What are you going to do about it?"

"I don't know yet. Right now, I am trying to make it through today."

"No wonder you have been so out of sorts. Promise me you won't tell Harry. It would kill him. Crystal is the apple of his eye."

"Fine with me."

"Hanging's too good for the scoundrel. Damn him!" To hear Mother cuss was as shocking as if the Pope had just said a swear word. People in her church would be stunned. Yet, they might understand if they heard what I just now told her.

"I can't hang Bart, but I am going to see my lawyer and divorce him."

In less than four hours, I signed my divorce papers in Greg's office. "I can have you on the Court Docket by June first."

"It can't happen until July first."

"Why is that?" He frowned.

"Bart may marry Rhonda. I'll be damned if she's going to be a June Bride. Not this year!"

"I understand. He should give you everything you want in the divorce settlement if he's smart."

"He's smart alright, too smart for his own good!"

✳ ✳ ✳

That afternoon, I drove to my real estate office to take phone time. In minutes my phone rang. A familiar voice screeched at me through the line. "What the hell makes you think I will give you the house, your car and pay all the bills in our divorce?"

"Be glad you aren't in prison."

"Why should I be there?"

"For what you did to Crystal. They call it incest!"

"I am not her father. He abandoned her when she was two. Tim adopted her, so he is her legal father not me!"

"We will see about that. You destroyed her life!"

"I'm not taking the blame for this!"

"Then who is?"

"Not me!" He slammed his phone in my ear.

His comments replayed in my weary head for hours. Around 4:50 a.m., I finally dozed off while sitting up listening to more sad country songs. My diet had improved to black licorice and bananas.

I woke up a few hours later and wondered about Stacy. I hadn't seen or heard from him in months. I had an aching Mother's need to see my son. The feeling gnawed at my heart. It is odd how ESP can work. In spite of the madness romping through my life, a small glimmer of hope eventually emerged. I woke up and wandered into the den.

Crystal was talking on the den telephone. She saw me and covered the mouthpiece. "This is Stacy. He misses us. I told him Bart is gone. He wants to move back home."

"He does?" The news shocked me. Happy tears flowed from a bottomless source. "Let me talk to him!" Crystal handed me the receiver. "Hi, honey, how are you?"

"I want to come home if Bart isn't coming back."

"It's no lie! He will not be back. I'll tell you why later. I am not surprised that you and Tim are not getting along."

"Mom, his drinking is too much."

"Where is Dana?"

"She's drunk every day when I come home from school."

"No wonder you want to come home." His news thrilled me. I hung up. The phone rang again. I thought it was Stacy. "What did you forget, honey?"

After a long silence, a whining voice spoke. "Kitten, I miss you. I want to come home."

"You must have lost your mind!" I shouted and hung up.

The phone rang again. I took a big breath and answered in a gruff voice. I figured it was Bart. "What is it?"

I startled Stacy. "Mom?"

"I'm sorry about that. Bart just called and upset me."

"Can I come home tonight?"

"Of course. Did something happen?"

"Dana is passed out in her room. Dad is passed out in his room. I want to come home right now. I'm just tired of this stuff! Do you mind?"

"Not at all. I'll be right over!" I hung up and asked Mother and Crystal to follow me in Momma's car. When we arrived at Tim's house, Stacy was waiting on the front porch with his bags. We quickly loaded his things into both cars and whisked him home.

That was the first time I had smiled in months. It made my heart sing to see my son back home in his room. Later, I kissed him goodnight in his room. He told me a surprising thing. "I never want to live with Dad again. I will sleep in the streets first!"

"I completely understand, honey. That's why I divorced him. You needed to find out for yourself what I put up with for almost five long years."

"How did you stand it?"

"It was difficult because of his drinking, yet I wanted you and Crystal to have a daddy."

That weekend lifted my spirits. I wanted to spend some meaningful time with my kids. As were leaving to see a movie and have dinner, Momma stopped me. "I must drive home to check on Harry. I will be back."

The following Monday, the kids returned to school. I went back to work at my real estate office. When I came home, Mother was already there to keep an *Eagle Eye* on me.

Later that afternoon, Stacy hurried in the front door. *"Mom, who does Bart know around the corner?"*

9

≈

Secrets That Stole My Life

Stacy explained. "I just saw Bart's Blazer and Rhonda's pickup park in a driveway four blocks from here. I went to Heritage Park after school and was on the swings, when I saw them drive up and go into a house."

"Maybe it belongs to one of Rhonda's friends. We don't know anyone on that street." I dismissed his information.

Before I left for work on Friday, Stacy sheepishly approached me in the den. "Mom, I think Bart and Rhonda are living in that house around the corner."

"Why do you think that?"

"I watched them carry boxes and furniture inside today."

"This cannot be happening!" I bristled and paced the floor. "He knows how much I hated it, when Tim lived only a few blocks from us. Why would he do this to me? I'll be right back!"

I grabbed my purse and ran out the front door to my Firebird. In seconds, my car practically flew west over the hill. I turned right at the corner. Sure enough, there sat Bart's Blazer and Rhonda's truck parked in front of a small gray house four blocks from my home. *Damn him to hell! When I drive to that corner, I will see their house, vehicles and maybe even them holding hands or kissing.*

Fury ripped through me. I stomped my gas pedal and whizzed toward their house. A For Rent sign was in the front yard. I jotted the phone number on some paper and rushed home to call the leasing agent. It was a co-worker in my real estate office.

"Bunny, this is Debbie. I see you are the leasing agent for a rent house on Forest Street. What is the name of the renters?"... "Mr. and Mrs. Bart Austin signed the lease?"

I dialed information. "Operator do you have a telephone listing on Forest Street for Bart Austin? ... Check for a Rhonda Marshall... Then try Rhonda Austin... I need that phone number." I jotted it number down and hung up. *"Damn that sorry bastard!"*

"What's the matter, hon'?" Mother had heard me.

"That rotten SOB moved in around the corner with Rhonda and her kids. Every time I go to the grocery store, I will see their house and vehicles. They are already calling themselves husband and wife. I just barely filed for divorce. This is so unfair." I flopped on the den couch. "Adelle always tells me, *nobody ever said life was fair!* I'm living proof of that."

Without warning, my flood of tears resumed. I rushed to the bedroom, slammed the door and cried for two solid hours. Finally, I heard a soft knock on my door. I pulled myself up and opened it.

"Can I talk to you for a minute?"

I motioned for Mother to enter and plopped on my bed.

"Honey, you must pull yourself together. These kids need you. I need you... Is there help of some kind like counseling or something? I'm worried about you."

"You're right. I feel so drained. I cannot seem to get to the bottom of these damned tears!" She squeezed my hand and returned to the den to get some sleep.

What is sleep? It is currently something that comes and goes like the wind. I couldn't sleep that night, so I sat up in bed and listened to a new song by The Eagles that sounded like Bart. It was "Desperado." *The words of their song described Bart to me.* A thunderstorm began to rumble outside.

At 3:00 a.m., the floodgate to my tears reopened. A rush of tears overwhelmed me. I stumbled to my bathroom and closed the door to muffle my loud sobs. I fell to my knees near the toilet and screamed hysterically at God. "Why did you do this to me? It is more than I can bear! You promised not to overburden me. *This is more than I can take! Why God? Why me?"*

Shrieking sobs rose from the depths of my wounded soul. I laid my head on my folded arms across the toilet seat lid. *God, where are you when I need you?*

Hours passed. I felt something, or someone, brush the hair from my swollen eyes. I felt certain an Angel came to comfort me, when I needed it most, and saw me through the long night. Otherwise, I should have died that night from a broken heart.

Morning arrived. A bright new day patiently awaited me. Noise from the nighttime thunderstorms and my agony had subsided. I woke up full of determination to make it. I flipped on my radio. Tammy Wynette's new country song was playing. *How poignant!* The title was "D-I-V-O-R-C-E."

A few days later, I searched for a counselor for Crystal and me. I located a County Medical Counselor named Annie Lane. She helped me a lot with my concerns. "Debbie, we share a similar concern over whether she is coping with the revelation of her sexual abuse. *Crystal must deal with her past eleven years, sooner or later."*

It took lots of work, but I finally convinced Crystal to visit Annie. They talked privately for one hour. I waited in the hallway.

Afterward, Annie invited me into her office. "Crystal seems to be perfectly fine."

"How can that happen?"

"She seems to be handling things amazingly good."

"How is that possible? She has been a victim of sexual abuse for over ten years. How could it not affect her?"

"From what I heard out of her, Crystal claims she has no problems from her abuse."

I drove Crystal home perplexed. How she could have no problems after being an abuse victim all that time? In my heart, I believed she wasn't honest with Annie.

✸ ✸ ✸

One day, I ran across a bottle of multi-colored pills stashed inside a bookshelf on Bart's side of the bed. I phoned Annie, described the pills, and she told me about each pill. "The black ones are Black Mollies; the yellow-and-black are Yellow Jackets; the big blue ones are Butterflies. It sounds like Bart has a significant drug problem."

"I am astounded. I find this difficult to believe."

At that moment, I re-affirmed my decision. *I must break up Bart and Rhonda any way I can to protect her children.* The fact that Bart was continually calling me, at all hours and crying and pleading to come home, should make it easy. He ends every phone call the same. "I love you, Debbie. I want to come home."

I woke up at five a.m., dolled myself up and put on one of Bart's Frederick's gifts hanging in my closet. I chose his favorite one with long red fringe, red feathers and red ribbon bows tied on each shoulder. I checked myself out in my closet door mirror and added high heels and flashy earrings. *This is the how Bart always wanted me to look.*

Quietly, I slipped on a lightweight long black jacket that I tied softly at my waist, grabbed my purse, car keys and eased out the front door, so I wouldn't wake up Crystal and Stacy.

Six blocks away, I parked my car near a four-way stop sign and waited. At 5:45 a.m., Bart's Blazer rolled down the long hill toward the stop sign. After he crossed the intersection, I pulled around the corner and flashed my lights. He turned into an apartment complex to park and walked to my car door. I rolled down my window and gave him a sensuous grin. "Got a minute, doll?"

"Sure, but I have to be at work by six-thirty."

"You live with the boss's daughter. He can cover for you!" I chided. "Get in!"

He walked around the front of my car. I could sense his uneasiness. For all he knew, I was about to correct my unfinished deed and blow his ass away with the Magnum he gave me when he left. He opened my passenger door and slid into the seat. "What's on your mind goodlookin'?"

"I decided I want you to come home. I miss you."

Bart sat there in disbelief for several moments. Finally, he arched his left eyebrow and leaned close. "Are you sure?"

"As sure as you are." I untied the loose belt on my black jacket and cocked my head. "I bet you've been thinking about this!" I took both hands, and I ever so slowly peeled my jacket away from my skimpily covered body.

It is moments like this, when I wish a movie camera was rolling. I would aptly label it "Get Even; Take One." The look on Bart's face was priceless. His nostrils began to flare. Of course, I added fuel to his fire. I slowly propped one knee on my console to fully expedite his sexual arousal.

"Well, goodlookin', our bed sure is lonely these nights." I purred like the kitten he wanted me to be and gently rubbed his arm. He leaned closer. I raised one eyebrow to steal his thunder. He looked like a dog in heat. His hand eagerly searched the borders of my soft thighs. I kept my mind focused on the hideous poem he wrote me on my birthday. *My Whispering Angel wanted me to see Bart's poem for an important reason. This must be why.*

I grabbed his left hand before he could violate the fringe on my red see-thru panties. "Easy there, tiger. I thought your poem said, 'Making love to me was like brushing your teeth.' "

"Oh kitten, I was on drugs when I wrote that. It was the drugs talking, not me."

"How often did you and Crystal smoke pot together?"

"I smoke pot a lot because it gives me sexual stamina. Many times, I would sit on top of the doghouse out back and smoke a joint. *Crystal would occasionally join me and take a puff or two of a joint.*"

Oh my God, I thought I knew my daughter. Even so, I remained determined to get Bart away from Rhonda's children at all cost. I sweetly convinced him to move into an apartment, so we could work things out and eventually get back together. It only took a week for Bart to move into an apartment. My plan was right on target.

✳ ✳ ✳

Bart rapidly invited me over to see his apartment. When I arrived, he was eager to show me his dwelling place. It had makeshift furniture he had borrowed from friends or bought at a Goodwill store, I guess. I no more than walked in, when his phone rang. I felt certain it was Rhonda by the way he shifted from foot-to-foot. It looked like he was standing on red hot coals! I smirked to myself. He hung up, and I took his hand. "We must talk about Rhonda. How can we work out our problems, if you are still seeing her?"

He gave me his perennial shoulder shrug. *I know how much Bart hates confrontations. He claims it comes from his tough childhood.*

"Come on. You know I'm right. Rhonda needs to stay out of this, or we can never work things out."

His warm lips met mine. I closed my eyes, imagined we were still together, and that the past four months were merely a garish nightmare. His eager fingers roamed inside my blouse. "Stay with me tonight kitten!"

"Quit changing the subject," I purred and moved his hand. "We must agree on Rhonda, or I am not coming back."

"Listen to me. She is history. I'll take care of her. Now, will you stay tonight?"

A thunderous series of raps pounded Bart's door. A familiar high-pitched voice called out. "Bart, let me in!"

"I need to go home."

"No, doll. I will tell her it's over right now! I promise."

"You would leave me in here?"

"It won't take long." He left and went out the door. Twenty minutes passed. I tired of the wait, pushed the door open, and startled them.

"Bye! I'm leaving."

"Debbie, wait up. I am about to walk Rhonda to her truck. I just explained to her that it's over."

"Really?" I paused to check her mood. She was wearing a fitting scowl along with her usual attire; tight blue jean shorts, white midriff blouse and those little girl dog-ears.

Bart took my hand and tugged. "Come with me. We can walk her to her truck."

She stomped along in front of us, as we escorted her to her pickup at the far end of the parking lot. We were an awkward looking trio that night. I felt sorry for Rhonda, and I also felt sorry for me. She burned rubber and sped her truck toward the street. I turned to Bart. "I need time to think things over. I must going home tonight."

He pleaded with me with his sad puppy dog eyes act. "I don't want to be alone tonight. Stay with me, hold me and nothing more. Please stay here tonight!"

"Very well, but nothing more!" I slept beside Bart with my clothes on all night and kept my left hand on my purse. I felt certain he wanted to steal my house keys.

Bart's alarm seemed to go off only seconds later. It was now five o'clock. I had unwillingly dropped off to sleep. He walked into the room already dressed for work and left for work. I pulled myself up and drove home to get some real sleep. Exhaustion became my middle name.

During the day, Bart called. "Come spend tonight with me."

"Not tonight. Another time." After the fourth call from him, I finally relented. "I guess."

I continued my crazy schedule for a week. In due time, I wore out and fell sound asleep for hours. I vaguely recall waking up and seeing a nude Bart standing in his small bathroom rummaging through my purse. I bolted up. "What are you looking for?"

"I have a sinus headache. I thought you might have some sinus pills."

"Let me find them!" I walked to his bathroom to reclaim my purse. After he left, I drove home and searched my purse. Items in my purse appeared intact. I wasn't sure what Bart wanted. Later it dawned on me. He could have traced the outline of my house keys on paper and asked a locksmith to make him a set of keys. *That does it! I have to change all the locks on my doors again. Damn the bastard!*

Before I did anything else, I purchased two new door locks and installed them myself, then I went my real estate office.

✳ ✳ ✳

Late that afternoon Stacy called. "Mom, you had a call from Grandma. She wants to talk to you."

I hung up and phoned Mother. "Why are you seeing Bart again after what he did to Crystal?"

"It's none of your business. I can handle things my way."

"How can you stand that man after what he did?"

"I will explain it to you later. Right now, I can't."

"You are playing with fire!"

"I know I am, but so is he."

The kids had to do their own cooking after that cold morning in March. My pots and pans began to gather dust. Before I left for Bart's apartment that night, I explained things to my kids. "Do not worry. Bart isn't coming home again, and there are plenty of microwave dinners in the icebox."

After I arrived at his apartment, he wanted to take me out to dinner. Afterward, we returned to his apartment at one a.m. We prepared for bed, when his phone rang. I could tell it must be Rhonda again. I heard him say, before he closed his bedroom door, "Don't cry, doll. It upsets me when you cry."

I waited until he returned to bed. "Who was on the phone?"

"Rhonda is upset. I calmed her down because she's drunk."

We drifted off to sleep. In short order, a deafening thud hit his door. This time it was one of his neighbors. "I need your help. A girl named Rhonda is in the parking lot threatening to shoot your truck!"

"That bitch!" He stepped into his jeans and boots and rushed outside. I decided to trace his door key and have a key made, in case I ever needed it. He returned an hour later. "What happened?"

"She was screaming at my truck and waving a shotgun. Neighbors called the cops. She smashed a camera I gave her and left."

Her overnight visit made me more than suspicious. I decided to do some checking. I drove to the street in front of Cotton's company where Bart worked. A coffee shop nearby caught my eye. I parked, went inside and asked for a seat with a street view, and I waited. As expected, his Blazer pulled away from the building and turned right at the corner. I caught a glimpse of Rhonda sitting in the front seat. I suppose her dark sunglasses are to keep anyone from recognizing her. *I would know those damned dog-ears anywhere. Rage whipped through me like a flashflood. I jumped to my feet. It was as if I had been shot through the heart one more time. That lying sack of shit! I should have known.* I rushed to my car and followed them. They stopped at Big Red's Bar.

At first, I considered dropping in to confront him. Instead, I stopped by a grocery store and had a key made from the tracing I did of his apartment key. I sped home and stormed in the front door. Crystal was in her bedroom talking on her phone.

"Get off the phone and come with me."

"What's wrong, Mom?"

"Crystal, we need to go someplace right now!"

10

≈

Time to Pull the Plug

I took Crystal by the hand. "We're going to the police station."

"Why?"

"Bart is completely hopeless. I thought I could get him away from Rhonda to protect her kids, after what he did to you. He's still seeing her. It is time to file charges on him! He has to be stopped before he hurts her children, too!"

Crystal hesitantly followed me to my car and climbed inside. I drove to the local police station across town and parked. I opened the heavy door of the one-story building and saw an officer sitting at a front desk. He appeared stunned, when I announced my reason for being there. *"I need to file a criminal charge."*

He stared at us for a few moments. "Just a minute. Have a seat." He pointed at four heavy wooden barrel chairs across the room. "Let me get a detective up here."

We sat down to wait. In minutes, he introduced us to Detective Powell. He escorted us to his office three doors down the marble hallway. The wall behind him had FBI Wanted posters and a large city and county map. His bare office window let in just enough light to see until dusk. Detective Powell was an attractive average-looking guy who would not stand out in a crowd. He sat behind his broad desk and motioned for us to be seated. "What can I do for you young ladies?"

"We're here to file criminal charges on my husband for sexual abuse."

"I see. Please go on." He began to take notes on a legal pad atop his cluttered desk.

Crystal sat beside me with her head bowed, as I related the ugly story about her years of hidden abuse by Bart. I described the picture album, large poster, pile of B&W 8x10's and her cigar box of handwritten sex stories I found on March 23rd.

"You have pictures. Is Bart Crystal's natural father?"

"No, but he raised her for eleven years. Why do you ask?"

"This sounds like a clear case of incest to me."

"Incest? Bart isn't her father."

"It does not matter. He was her legal caretaker for eleven years as your husband. In the eyes of the law, that is incest."

I looked at Crystal. She was staring at her lap. *I presume she disappeared into a Black Hole for refuge.*

Detective Powell gazed at Crystal. "Young lady, we can't go any further without your help."

"Crystal, Detective Powell is talking to you."

She stammered. "What did you say?"

Detective Powell repeated. "We cannot go any further without your testimony. Will you testify in court?" He tried to look into her downcast eyes.

"Yeah. I guess so."

"Are you sure? I hear a question mark."

"I'm sure." She nodded.

He turned to me. "I need to see those pictures and other items as quick as possible. Crystal needs to feel completely comfortable. We have a female officer next door who will interview her."

We waited for Crystal to agree to the interview. I turned to her. "What do you think, sweetie? Shall we go ahead or not?"

Detective Powell interrupted. "Mrs. Austin, Crystal, these cases are not easy. I mean they will... to put it bluntly, these kinds of cases are tough for a victim. Bart's defense attorney will interrogate you. It will be hard-hitting!" Detective Powell paused for her final decision.

I knew what I wanted, yet the final decision rested with Crystal. She is the person that Bart secretly violated all those years. If she refuses, then I must respect her decision. I sensed her fear and closed my eyes. She finally nodded. "I'll do it."

"Thank goodness!" Detective Powell grinned. "Crystal, follow me. Officer Bolling will interview you, while I get information from your mom." He escorted her out the door and quickly returned. "Now, Mrs. Austin, I need all the facts about..."

It took over an hour for each of us to tell our story, about the past eleven years, to each officer. Afterward, Detective Powell walked us to the front door of the police station. "All I need are those photos and anything else you found to build our case."

"I will bring them tomorrow. They're well hidden. I can easily retrieve them."

"Mighty fine." He turned to Crystal. "Young lady, you just did a very brave thing."

I nodded. "She certainly did."

We both knew we had made a dangerous decision about Bart. On the way home, Crystal worried aloud. "Mom, what will Bart do?"

"I'm not sure, sweetheart. Who knows?"

Come morning, I phoned Adelle before she left for work. "I need to drop by and get Bart's white satchel and stuff from you."

At first she hesitated, until I explained my reason. By eleven a.m., I was sitting at Detective Powell's desk holding the white satchel contents and the big poster in my lap. I removed Crystal's cigar box, showed him the sex bondage stories Crystal wrote to Bart, one letter he wrote to her, and his sickening poem that he wrote to me on my birthday. I handed him the Family Album, a huge envelope of 8x10 B&W nude photos of Crystal that Bart had stuffed inside the satchel, the cigar box with Crystal's sex stories and the rolled-up poster. He looked through several album pages of Crystal's photos. "Any shots in here with Bart in the picture?"

"There's only this one." I showed him the most crucial photo evidence. It was a shot of the back of Bart's head and shoulders. *Crystal took it of his nude body, while he was on his knees pleasuring her orally.* Momentarily, I shut down and withdrew. *Does she hate me that much?*

"We have plenty of evidence with this one picture. Plus, with everything you brought here today and Crystal's testimony, we should have all we need." He sighed. "I must keep these items for a while. Then you can put them back in safekeeping."

For a moment, Detective Powell appeared to drift into serious thought. "Damn him. I have a daughter the same age as Crystal. He is one lucky guy that you didn't shoot him that morning in his sleep. I'm not sure I could have stopped myself, if I'd found out something like this about my daughter."

"And now, he has his hands on another lady with two kids the same age as mine were when we married. What happens next?"

"A sheriff will serve him with a Criminal Subpoena tomorrow to appear in County Court. He will face charges of incest, and you and Crystal must go before the Grand Jury and testify, for us to get an indictment. Once that's done, the court sets a trial date. Then it is up to a judge and jury." He shrugged. "We never know, until we get a verdict, how these cases will end. This one is a fairly pat case with all your evidence. What is missing is anything verbal like a tape. Is there a possibility you could tape him without him knowing it? I want you to ask him why he did it and some other details."

"If do this, it must be tonight, before he's served with papers tomorrow. Yes, I can do it. I will bring it to you early tomorrow morning."

"Great! Then he will be signed, sealed, and delivered!"

I thanked him, drove home and phoned Bart. I used my best fake ultra-sexy voice. "Hi there, what's happening? ... You know I missed seeing you yesterday, and you never called. Why not you come by the house tonight? The last time you were here was last March... Stacy and Crystal have plans to go to a birthday party at the skating rink tonight... See you about seven p.m."

✳ ✳ ✳

It should be easy to convince Stacy and Crystal to go skating tonight. First, I must buy a tape recorder with a blank tape and hide it near the end of the den couch.

The kids were eager to go skating. I felt Crystal needed to keep her mind occupied, after the emotional events of yesterday. I watched them drive away and went to Radio Shack to buy a recorder and a blank tape. I hurried home to set everything up in the den and ran a couple of tests. It is imperative that I know the recorder can hear us talking. I placed it under the couch and grew nervous when it failed to work.

What will I do now? I must think like a criminal to outsmart Bart, or he will spot this recorder. Careful is the word. I calmed myself down and discovered it worked nicely on my French provincial end table beside the couch. I hid it under the partial half-shelf and covered it with a linen cloth. It looked totally inconspicuous.

At seven p.m., Bart rang the doorbell. I turned on the recorder, answered the door and led him inside. I fixed him a cup of hot coffee and sat it on the edge of the coffee table in front of our blue couch. The hidden recorder was rolling.

I purposely wore a short white skirt and a pink see-through blouse, to keep his eyes completely focused on me. Then I carefully steered the conversation toward a discussion about Crystal and the past eleven years. For over an hour, Bart gave me blow-by-blow details about his intimate sexual activities with my daughter, since the day we were married eleven years ago.

The asshole can't wiggle out of this one. I have him by his balls, and he is oblivious to it. I smirked to myself.

Bart described times when I did yard work. They would be in our living room, where he took nude shots of her. If I went grocery shopping, he took pictures of her on our bed doing sexual acts. Later that evening, he would ask me to do the same thing and take similar photos. I never dreamed he had done the same thing earlier with my daughter.

"What about the nude photo of Crystal in my red fox coat?"

"It was her idea."

"Who wanted to take the picture of her spread-eagle on top of our pool table using a dildo?"

"Also her idea. Occasionally, I would ground her from her social activities, if she refused to do what I wanted sexually. Other times, I might threaten to tell Eric about us."

"Was that white picture album always in your Blazer?"

"I always kept it in my bedroom closet. For some unexplainable reason, I decided to move it to my Blazer the day before you found it."

More proof that God sent an Angel to whisper in my ear on that cold morning. "Go! Look in the truck!" My Angel was watching over me.

"Often times, we made out in the tool shed. Other days, Beulah and I made out in the swimming pool or a hotel room. I photographed her a lot. She finally demanded that I give her the pictures, but I made copies of them first."

When I asked another question, I encountered even more heart-wrenching details. "Where was Crystal when she wrote those sex stories that I found inside her Tampa Nugget cigar box with her printed name on the top?"

"She wrote them at school while she was in study hall. They were explicit sexual encounter stories she would dream up and want to do with me. She loved to read them to me in our bed. It got me good and horny. That is how she likes me the best."

I hoped that his ugly revelations were finally at an end, until he tossed out another unsolicited admission. "Most of her so-called kid spankings were phony. We would sit behind our closed bedroom door and try not to laugh too loud. She would pretend my spanking was hurting her. We always faked the whole thing.

It was difficult to maintain my self-control at that point and not do something stupid. I managed to control my anger, because I knew the tape recorder was documenting everything he just said.

I was not ready for the most disgusting part of our chat. Bart planted huge seeds of doubt in my mind about Crystal's part in their relationship. "She enjoyed me and loved our kinky sex. She never wanted it to end and... She loves me, and I love her."

As his conversation ended, my wounds were deeper than ever. *His last admission about Crystal cut me to the quick. Can his claim be true? Is my daughter in love with my husband?*

Never one to miss an opportunity, Bart invited me to spend the night with him. I put on my best act of the night and permitted him to have sex with me one last time on our back porch. Indeed, it was to be the last time! Our sex had nothing to do with making love. My mission remained to protect Rhonda's two innocent children and get evidence for a Grand Jury indictment. *The part about Bart and Crystal being in love makes my skin crawl. Surely, he has to be lying!*

A sick smirk of secret satisfaction dressed his face, as he peeled off his clothes. I looked at him honestly for the first time in my life. I saw a thin framed, awkward hipped, sunken eyed, short man with a crooked nose. I slept with this man for eleven years. Today, he resembles a demonic scarecrow. The sex was not the least bit pleasurable for me. I faked the hell out of it. I pretended enjoyment and a noisy climax.

Afterward, I walked him to the door, patted his scrawny ass and shot back one of his favorite lines. "Not bad for a white boy."

We said goodbye at the front door. I walked down the hallway and took a scorching hot bath to rid my body of his fingerprints. I brushed my teeth and spoke to the strained face staring at me in the mirror. *"Sex with you, Mr. Snake Charmer, was like brushing my teeth. Tomorrow you'll be in for one hell of a big shock, you bastard!"*

✻ ✻ ✻

Our airplane suddenly lurched. I closed the book, left it on my seat and headed to the restroom. Someone tapped my shoulder. I turned to see the stewardess, as she leaned close and whispered, "Who could blame Crystal for going into porn, after what she lived through?"

I gritted my teeth in deep compassion for Debbie Austin. "I guess not." Then I entered an available restroom door. As I exited, the stewardess handed me a Kleenex. *I didn't realize I was crying profusely.* I returned to my seat, stared at the book and drifted off to sleep for an hour. Suddenly, the plane hit extremely rough weather and woke me up. I tightened my seatbelt. Once the plane stopped rocking, I reopened Debbie Austin's book.

✳ ✳ ✳

I grabbed Bart's confession tape and was about leave for Detective Powell's office, when Stacy pulled me aside. "Mom, I have been thinking about things. There is something I need to say."

"What is that honey?"

"Remember that water fountain Bart started to build you in the backyard?"

"I sure do. He started it, and he never finished it."

"Because Crystal told him not to finish it."

"How do you know that?"

"More than once, I overheard her tell him, 'Forget it.' "

"Why would she do that, Stacy? She knows how much I wanted a water fountain."

"I have no idea, Mom."

Stacy's revelation left me speechless. Who is my daughter? The more I hear, the more I feel like I never knew her at all.

Then Stacy unloaded another tidbit that shocked me even more. "I saw Bart in bed with Crystal one morning. That is why he hit me with my trashcan and hurt my arm. He wanted to scare me, so that I wouldn't tell you that I saw them in bed together."

✳ ✳ ✳

I left the tape with Detective Powell and paused outside the police station. *What else did Crystal tell Bart not to do? Maybe somewhere I wanted to go or an extra special place to visit?*

On *June 16, 1981*, Sheriff Jackson served Bart with a Criminal Subpoena to appear in the Justice Court. The DA charged Bart with Criminal Incest in The State vs. Bart Austin.

I drove to work at my real estate office that afternoon to take phone time for property calls. Within minutes, my phone rang. "This is Debbie. May I help you?"

A vicious voice surged through my telephone line. "What the fucking hell do you think you're doing, bitch?"

"Preventing you from hurting any more children!"

"I never hurt Crystal. She liked what I did. She craved me. I wanted her as much. Otherwise, she would have told you what I was doing!" He just successfully planted more seeds of doubt, in my already wavering mind, about Crystal's role in this whole mess. Even now, he was not through. "I did nothing wrong. I'm not her dad."

That was an As the Knife Turns moment for me. I refused to back down from his denial and lies. "You should have thought about the consequences before you started abusing her eleven years ago. You helped me raise her."

"If you and Crystal refuse to drop those charges, the house might accidentally burn down or something horrible could happen to the three of you very unexpectedly."

"I tell you what, hotshot. Arrangements have been made. If anything happens to me, the kids, or our house, you're a dead man!"

"You can't scare me. Drop those charges or fucking else!"

"Go to Hell!" I heard myself scream, before I slammed my phone. *At that point, I feared nothing and no one. Bart stripped me of all reason to live. Stupidly, he had yet to discover just how unpredictable and totally dangerous I was at that moment.*

Mrs. Janski walked past my office and apparently heard the last part of my conversation with Bart. "Debbie, what's happening?"

"Crystal is going to testify against Bart. The Grand Jury just served him with papers charging him with incest."

"Oh honey, be careful. He is so dangerous!"

"I can take care of myself!" I assured her. "Right now, I need to go home and talk to my kids."

✳ ✳ ✳

I sat Stacy and Crystal down in the den. "We have to be extremely cautious. Bart just made some serious threats against us."

Crystal was silent. Stacy was my instant hero. "Mom, I have a knife Bart gave me and a B.B. gun."

At five p.m., Eric arrived to see Crystal. I pulled him aside and privately explained our dilemma. "I need for you to do three things for me. Promise me, if anything happens to us or our home, that you'll find someone to take care of Bart. Also, will you stay here for a week and sleep on our couch. Lastly, I am going to buy three new door locks. I need your help to install them."

Eric erupted in anger. "If he hurts any of you I have connections. They will do more than break his legs. Don't worry about him. Now, what caused this to happen?"

"I prefer Crystal tell you, if she will."

"I'm going home to get my shotgun, more clothes and my drill. I will be right back." He raced out the front door.

I went to my bedroom, loaded my Magnum with hollow point bullets and eased the gun inside my purse. This baby is one heavy piece.

I heard Eric return and approached him. "Stay here with Crystal and Stacy. Don't answer the door or the phone, until I get back."

When I returned, Eric and Crystal were talking in her bedroom. Eric looked shaken as he entered the den to install our new door locks. My phone rang. It was John Scherer, our new next door neighbor. He was a nice chatty guy with a graying beard.

"Debbie, it's your new kid on the block, John. Bart came by tonight for a chat. I picked up bad vibes from him. I thought you needed to know."

"Thanks. Precautions are in play." Then I hung up. That night, Eric slept on the couch with a loaded shotgun on the floor beside him. I paced the floor most of the night, between my bedroom and our bay window, to watch for signs of trouble. None appeared.

I only left the house to go to work or buy food for two days. My Magnum was tucked in my purse. I envisioned Bart would stalk me eventually and try something. On the third day, he called the house twice and my real estate office three times. Each call was the same message. "Drop those criminal charges or else!"

Out of caution, I decided to stay home that night. Both phones remained silent. Eric continued to ride shotgun on our den couch. I sat beside him. "Bart called me five times today."

"Then I want to spend another week on your couch."

At three a.m., he fell asleep in an upright position with his shotgun across his lap. I finally fell asleep on my bed. Early Wednesday morning, Stacy hurried into my bedroom. "Mom, where's your car?"

"Out front behind Crystal's car."

"I don't see it."

"You have got to be kidding! It has to be there!" I dashed to Crystal's room and peered out her window. No car. I grabbed the phone and dialed the police. "I need to report a stolen car... I know it's stolen because it's gone. I didn't move it... Yes, my husband has a key. We're getting a divorce... You want me to call him? Why can't you do it? ... This is a domestic problem? Okay, let me call him, and I will call you back." I pushed the receiver button for a dial tone and phoned Bart at work.

"Hello Justine, is Bart there? ... How did he get there? ... He rode with you and Rob. Where is his truck? ... Parked at his apartment... Can I speak to him? ... What the hell did you do with my car? ... You are lying, asshole... Someone stole my car. I know you took it... Bullshit! Your word means nothing to me!"

Evil laughter shot through the telephone line and left no room for doubt. Bart stole my car! I called the police and spoke to the same officer. "Yes, he denied stealing my car... He's lying. I want him arrested... It isn't car theft? Why not? ... My car is community property until our divorce is final? ... Does that mean he can come over here and steal everything I own, and you can't help me? ... Then, the same thing applies to me?"

The officer confirmed my assessment. I hung up the phone receiver. My wheels began to spin ninety-miles-an-hour. I stormed to the den. "Eric, wake up. We are going to Bart's apartment right now!"

He gathered his wits. *"Now why are we going to Bart's apartment?"*

11

≈

One Fearless Pissed Off Bitch

"You'll see, Eric!" I fumed, hurried to John's door and rang his doorbell. "Have a minute?"

"Sure!" He stepped onto his front porch and peered over his gold-rimmed glasses. "What's up kid?"

"Bart threatened to burn down my home and kill all of us. I am carrying my Magnum everywhere. I have already changed my door locks several times. This morning he stole my car. The police refused to help because our divorce is not final."

"Good grief!"

"Will you do me a huge favor?"

"Sure! What is it?"

"I want you to rent a U-Haul truck and meet me at Bart's apartment. I can pay you later." He nodded. I handed him the address. "Thanks a million!" I rushed home to find Eric. Mother drove up unexpectedly. I turned to greet her as Eric barreled out the front door. "Okay, let's do this!"

He was halfway across the front sidewalk, when Mother stepped out of her black Impala. "Momma, I need to borrow your car. Bart stole my Firebird. No one will know me in your car."

Obediently, she handed me her keys. "Be careful, honey."

Eric slid into the passenger seat. I hurried behind the wheel. "We're off kiddo!"

During the drive, I explained my plan to Eric. "We are going to steal Bart's truck and clean out his apartment!"

"Wow!" He beamed. "Isn't that illegal?"

"Not according to the police. He can steal my car, so I can steal his truck, but I want to do him one better. We'll take all of his furniture. My neighbor just left to rent a U-Haul truck."

"How can we get into his truck and his apartment?"

"I will find a locksmith." I turned the Impala left and entered his apartment driveway to find Bart's Blazer. He had parked it on the north side of their U-shaped lot. I jumped out to check the doors. All doors were locked. He never gave me a key.

I entered Mother's car and took off toward a nearby business district. Within in blocks, I spotted a small stand-alone locksmith shop and whipped her car into the driveway. Just then, a young man wearing a red bandanna walked around the corner and unlocked the front door. His shaggy beard, long hair, worn blue jeans and green plaid shirt said he was someone with an open mind.

"Hi there. I need to hire a locksmith."

"I'm your man!" He grinned.

"Can you get me into a locked truck?"

"In less than two seconds."

"Can you start a truck up without keys?"

"Yeah, but that takes a couple of minutes more. Why do you need to do that?"

"I have an enormous problem. I am getting a divorce. My husband stole my car last night. The police will not help me. They say that my car is still community property, until we're divorced."

"You don't say." He looked at me with a puzzled gaze.

"It that means, I can steal his truck, and it isn't theft. He took my car and refuses to tell me where it is."

"I rather not get involved."

"Listen. He threatened to burn down my home and kill me and my two kids."

"Why are you messin' with him?"

"Because he sexually abused my teenage daughter for the past eleven years. We just filed incest charges against him!"

My comment struck a nerve with the young man. Instantly, he was sympathetic and ready to help me.

"Where is his truck?"

"Five blocks from here."

"Let's go!" He locked his door and turned his sign to Closed.

Eric and I stepped into Mother's car. The locksmith brought his toolbox and sat in the backseat. I sped north to his apartment. John was waiting with a big U-Haul truck out front. I stopped beside it. Eric rolled down his window. "Way to go, John. Wait here until we get the Blazer off the lot!"

He nodded. I drove toward the Blazer and parked beside it. The locksmith took his toolbox and entered the Blazer in thirty seconds. He quickly removed Bart's steering wheel.

Eric waved his hands. "We have been spotted!" He pointed at an apartment manager walking along the side of the complex.

"No, we haven't. She kept walking." I decided to get in the Blazer and left Eric in Mother's car.

The locksmith heard me tap on the passenger window and let me inside. "What's the problem now?"

"I am unable to get through the base of the steering column to hot wire the ignition."

"What will we do?"

"Improvise. A screwdriver in the ignition should work."

Eric climbed out of Mother's car and tapped my window. "Hey, we need to get out of here. The manager just walked by again. I think she spotted us!"

"No, she hasn't, or she would have called the police. I still want all of his furniture in the U-Haul. The locksmith is almost finished."

"Forget his blasted furniture!" Eric began to shake.

"No way. I want it all!" I turned to the locksmith. "How is it coming?"

"Takin' longer than I thought. I can make it!" He grinned and kept on working.

Eric was a basket case. "I have a bad feeling about that manager. What if she called Bart, and he's on his way?"

"Calm down. I told you, 'I want it all!' "

Six minutes passed. The apartment manager walked along the building sidewalk a third time. The locksmith shouted. "I did it! Now, where is his apartment door?"

I made a split-second decision. "I better not press my luck. I say we take the Blazer, and forget the furniture."

Eric whispered through my open window. "Hallelujah!" He drove Mother's car off the lot. The locksmith drove me and the Blazer to the front street and stopped.

I hopped out to update John. "I decided not to take the furniture. Return the U-Haul. I will pay you later."

John drove north. We drove south to the locksmith's shop. I went inside to pay him and realized another dilemma. "Gosh! Where can I hide this enormous Blazer, so that Bart will never find it?"

"No problem. This guy knows just the place. That pervert will never find it in a million years. Follow me!"

We trailed the locksmith's truck to his older home across town. I backed the Blazer into his well-fenced backyard. His towering trees will provide a perfect umbrella-like cover.

I grinned at Eric. "With these tall trees, Bart couldn't spot his Blazer with a helicopter!"

The locksmith closed his tall chain link gate, snapped a padlock shut and let his two chow dogs outside. *"My dogs don't like child abusers either!"*

On the way back to his shop, the locksmith tapped my shoulder. "You can leave his truck there as long as you need, at no cost!"

"I couldn't have planned it better myself!" I shook his hand. In no time, we arrived at his shop. "I want to thank you for your help." I gave him a nice tip.

"No, need Ma'am. It was my pleasure."

When Eric and I arrived at my home, Mother met us at the front door. "Where have you been? I have been worried to death."

"We stole Bart's truck and hid it. I bet I get my car now!"

Mother was speechless. She just shook her head.

It tickled Stacy that I outsmarted Bart. "Way to go, Mom!" Crystal remained strangely silent.

I felt confident and borrowed her car to take phone time at my real estate office, after I changed clothes. Torrential rain made the drive to the office extremely difficult. I was not looking forward to showing property in bad weather. I no more than sat down when my desk phone rang.

"Where the hell's my damn truck?"

"Where the hell is my damn car?"

"How should I know?"

"How should I know what happened to your damn truck?"

"I will turn you in to the police!"

"You go ahead. They'll tell you the same thing they told me. 'Tough stuff!' "

"I'll find my truck, and you will be sorry as hell!"

"I don't have your precious truck, asshole!"

A jarring bolt of lightning shot through the outside air at the same moment that Bart slammed his phone in my ear.

✳ ✳ ✳

Mother soon returned home to check on Harry. The heavy rains flooded the city every day. My phone suddenly rang off the wall. Adelle called first. "Someone busted my car windshield. Do you think it was Bart?"

Then Mother phoned. "Debbie, a brick broke Harry's truck windshield."

Later, I drove to the real estate office. Mrs. Janski pulled me aside. "Debbie, a huge rock broke my bay window last night. It had to be Bart."

Eric phoned me later. "That SOB shot up my new pickup truck door with a B.B. gun last night."

Three evenings passed. Bart parked Rhonda's truck in front of John's house. Rhonda was with him. John happened to see Bart and engaged him in conversation to see what was happening.

John called me after they went back to her truck. "I caught Bart just now in-between my house and Beulah's house."

"Did he say what he wanted?"

"He said very little, except he asked if I'd seen his Blazer."

"Well, well, well, somebody is getting desperate."

I phoned the police and explained to an officer the seriousness of the situation. "I'm involved in a divorce with Bart. He has been stalking me, my family and doing damage to many people's property."

"You can get a Peace Bond, but it is as worthless as the paper it's written on. We are unable to enforce it, until he hurts you, your kids or someone else."

"Yeah, and by then it will be too late!"

"Correct. We can drop by to see him. Is he still there?"

"Yes. Come on over!"

Two officers arrived in minutes. I peered out the bay window and watched them talk to Bart and Rhonda. Light rain began to fall. Minutes later everyone left.

Early the next morning, the sun was shining for the first time in a week. Mother returned that afternoon just as my home phone rang. A frail little voice whined. "I want my truck back!"

"First you return my car. Then I give you your truck!"

"I have looked everywhere. I can't find it!"

"I told you, 'I hid it too well.' "

"I want to know how you did that and where you hid my truck. This is not like you!"

"I learned from a master. You taught me too well!"

"So be it. I give up. Just give me my truck!"

"First, I get my car!"

"Only if you and Crystal meet with me first."

"Why should Crystal be there?"

"I miss her. I want to see her."

"I doubt she wants to see you!"

"Oh, she will come!" He assured me. "Meet me across from the Quality Inn at Sonny's Restaurant tomorrow at nine a.m."

"I'll be there."

"Bring Crystal and directions to my truck."

"Tomorrow it is." I hung up and went to find Crystal. She was outside sunning by our pool. I walked out the back door. "Crystal, do you want to go with me tomorrow to meet Bart and get my Firebird?"

"Sure." Her nonchalant response bothered me.

"Are you sure?"

"You'll be there, so why not?"

Crystal's cavalier reply didn't set well with me.

✻ ✻ ✻

The next morning, and against Mother's objections, I drove us to Sonny's in Crystal's car. We could see Bart inside waiting in a red booth. We walked in and sat down. He greeted Crystal first and then me. I watched her give him a big warm smile. It made me mad. I saw no exploding rage toward the man she claims stole her innocence. Instead, there was nothing except happy smiles between the two of them. Her behavior toward Bart does not compute.

"Where's my car?"

"First, where is my truck?"

"You either do what you agreed to do, or we are gone!"

"Calm down. Here are your keys." He slid his copy of my keys across the table.

"Now, where is my car?"

"It is right across the street." He pointed at the *Quality Inn.* "Your car was there all the time. And my truck?"

"I have to get it. It isn't where you can locate it."

"Don't I know it? You must have stashed it in someone's warehouse."

"The location is none of your business. I will give you directions. You can call me tonight."

"You're tough. I don't know you anymore."

"Thanks to you, I am now tough as nails."

He reached for Crystal's hand. "How have you been doing?"

I fumed. "Let's go Crystal!" She smiled at Bart, stood up, and we left. I drove her car across the street and saw my Firebird sitting in plain sight waiting for me. My heart sank when I opened my driver door. I found two inches of water in both front floorboards. The heavy downpours from the past week, and a mysterious windshield leak that my car didn't have before Bart stole it, left me upset again.

Crystal found a beach towel in her trunk. I used an empty cup to bail water. We managed to remove most of it before we left. It felt fantastic to have my wheels back, water and all. Crystal followed me home in her car.

After we arrived, I phoned the locksmith and set up a time to retrieve the Blazer. Next, I called Eric. "Can you come over here right now and go with me? I have my car back. I need to retrieve Bart's Blazer."

"You bet!"

Eric arrived in his truck and drove me to the locksmith shop. Then he drove me and the locksmith to his house to get the Blazer. I drove it back to the shop and parked alongside the locksmith's small building. Eric and the locksmith arrived, and he parked his truck. The locksmith re-opened his shop. While I rummaged through the Blazer for a few things, Eric took a B.B. gun from his truck and shot Bart's door over twenty times. "Take that, Mr. Smart Guy!"

I laughed. "That'll teach him!"

Next, I gave the locksmith a nice reward for helping me out. Then I drove the Blazer east to find a place to park it. Eric followed in his truck. I spotted a cul-de-sac lined with two-story duplex apartments, parked the Blazer, locked the doors, jumped in Eric's truck, and he drove me home.

"Would you mind sleeping on the couch tonight? I feel that Bart may try something else."

"You know I will."

When we walked inside, I phoned Bart at work. "I parked your Blazer at 544 Parker Court."

"I don't know that street?"

"Look it up on a map."

I put all thoughts of the Blazer aside. Later the phone rang. Bart was drunk as a skunk. "I'm lost. Where is my Blazer?"

Mr. Badass sounds like a drunk whimpering child on the phone. Clearly, he wants my sympathy. He came to the wrong gal. "I gave you the address, now leave me alone!" I hung up on him.

The phone rang again. "I can't find it. Help me."

"Let Rhonda help you find it."

"She and her brother are passed out. They are passed out!"

"Where are you?"

"At her house around the corner."

"I guess so." I hung up and woke Eric. "Will you accompany me, while I take Bart to his truck? It isn't safe for me to be alone with him."

Eric sat up on the couch and rubbed his eyes. "Let's go."

We took Mother's car because it had a large backseat. I wanted distance between us and Bart. I drove over the hill, turned the corner and there was Bart all decked out in his finest boots, hat, shirt, jeans and western belt. We spotted him weaving beneath a streetlight. Eric and I cracked up. He was a comical sight to see.

Eric rolled down his window. Butter could have melted in Bart's mouth. "I love you, Debbie." Even across the front seat, the smell of alcohol on his breath made me gag.

"Get in the backseat!"

It reminded me of those sickening days with Harry. I drove Bart to his truck, and we returned to my home.

✳ ✳ ✳

Detective Powell called me that afternoon. "The Grand Jury has requested that you and Crystal testify before them tomorrow. We need an indictment on the incest charges. Meet me on the fourth floor of the County Courthouse at ten a.m."

"We will be there!" I hung up. Then it rang again.

"Debbie, this is Jerry Kahn. I understand you and Crystal will testify before the Grand Jury tomorrow. I want to visit with both of you in my office before then. Can you be here tomorrow at nine a.m.?"

"Why should we do that?"

"I want to prepare you and Crystal for what I will say in court, if Bart gets indicted. Can you be here?"

"I suppose?" I hung up. Is there a full moon tonight?

Mother walked down the hallway with her bags. "I need to go home. Harry called me today. He says that he's lonely."

"I understand. Let me put your bags in your car." I loaded her bags in her backseat, just as Eric and Crystal parked behind her car. Stacy was in their back seat. They had been at Tim's house to pick up Stacy's movie posters. Most of them were from the *Rocky Horror Picture Show.*

After Mother left, I went inside. Stacy was busy hanging posters in his room. Crystal and Eric followed me to the den.

"Detective Powell phoned. The Grand Jury wants to talk with us in the morning to decide whether or not they will indict Bart. His lawyer also called. He wants us to stop by his office first thing tomorrow."

Crystal's big eyes grew even wider. "Why does he want to see us?"

"To explain how he plans to defend Bart's case."

Silence filled the room. Each of us pondered the unknown. The lawyer strategy behind Jerry Kahn's brazen phone call.

Crystal finally looked at me with grim determination. "Then we must go see him!"

I hugged her. "That's my girl!"

Eric wrapped his arm around her shoulders. "Babe, I want to go with you as support. I'd like to castrate that scumbag!"

Crystal seemed more in control than both of us. "What's for dinner, Mom?"

"Your choice, honey. I have steak and baked potatoes, or we can eat out."

"I want steak and baked potatoes with lots of sour cream, butter, and bacon bits."

Eric unexpectedly took off while I cooked supper. He returned in twenty minutes and surprised Crystal with red roses and a card. *"Babe, I love you. I will be with you through the storm. Love Always, Eric!"*

When I realized what he'd done, I almost cried. We sat down to eat, conversation was tough, given the magnitude of the next day.

✳ ✳ ✳

The clock rushed forward to the next morning. We left Stacy at home redecorating his room. The three of us headed downtown in my car.

Jerry Kahn smiled as we sat down in his office. "Debbie, Crystal, and...?"

"Eric Keys, Crystal's boyfriend."

Jerry addressed Crystal first. "I will get right to the point. Both of you are about to appear before the Grand Jury this morning. Bart could be indicted on incest charges. If he is indicted, I will defend him. You will not like my presentation."

I snapped. "That's no surprise."

"First, I will interrogate this young lady unmercifully about her personal sex life, her choice of friends, and her manner of dress. Things like, have you ever smoked pot; ever do drugs and been dusted; ever shoplifted? I will use anything in court, and I will not be kind. I will be so cruel that you will wish you had never met me. Can you handle my embarrassingly brutal questions, young lady?"

Crystal remained silent.

"The media will somehow be notified about the trial by an anonymous tipster. The case will likely make both local newspapers, and you know how the media can misquote everything. Crystal, your friends, neighbors and relatives will read all about your sordid little life. You don't want that, do you?" He stared at her with overly callous eyes.

Crystal's head dropped. She stared at the white dots on her blue skirt. Eric doubled up his fists. My jaw tightened like a vice. "Lawyers can be sued!"

Jerry ignored my comment. *"Crystal, your handwritten BDSM stories will be one of my prime exhibits. They show your consent and willingness to have all kinds of sex."* He smirked, leaned back in his cushy chair and gazed at the ceiling for a long moment.

✳ ✳ ✳

I studied body language in real estate. His shoulder shrug indicated, "I have it made." The leaning back pose, "This is a take it or leave it deal." His gaze at the ceiling, "I am talking over their heads, so I'll make them sweat." For his finale, he rolled his gold pin over-and-over across his desk. "This case is all sewn up before it even starts."

✳ ✳ ✳

Jerry was far from finished. "Bart will plead innocent, and he will walk."

"Innocent my ass!" Eric cried out.

"Bart's in a picture. I secretly taped his admission of guilt. There is no way he can get out of this one!"

"His best friend, Gus Hurst, agreed to swear that he is the man in that photo. There is no visible face, only the back of a male's head and shoulders."

"Gus would never do that! He knows it's a lie!"

Jerry opened his desk drawer and tossed out an envelope. "Inside that envelope is a sworn statement by Gus that he is the person in question. He stated that Crystal willingly had sex with him."

"She is still in her teens!"

"Correct, and her willingness is most apparent in that stack of letters to Bart which date back over four years. *Did you miss her letter where she gushed about an upcoming ménage à trois?* In the eyes of the law, that statement makes her more than a willing participant."

Eric jumped to his feet. "I will not listen to any more of your lies!"

"It's time to go, Crystal." I stood up. Crystal didn't move.

"Come on, honey, let's go meet Detective Powell. We wasted our time being here today."

Jerry had planted countless seeds of doubt in Crystal's mind and also in mine. Before we left, I challenged Jerry in private. "How could you do this to my daughter?"

"I see things like this go on all the time. It could be a lot worse than what happened to Crystal!"

"How could anything be worse than this?"

"In the next room sits a preacher who molested his own son." His story left me speechless...

✳ ✳ ✳

At the courthouse, Detective Powell led us through a doorway and into a waiting room to testify before the Grand Jury. Eric stayed in the hall. Crystal was cool as a cucumber as we waited.

Shortly, Detective Powell opened the door. "Come with me, Crystal." He led her through a wooden door with a milky glass window insert and into a smoke-filled room. I stared at the big black letters printed on the door, *Grand Jury Room.*

Crystal stayed gone for fifteen minutes. When she returned, Detective Powell came out and waved. "You can both go now."

"I thought I had to testify?"

"The Jury Foreman said that Crystal was quite convincing. We'll know something in a few days. I will call you, when their list of indictments comes out."

An air of nervous relief filled my car, as I drove us home. Eric and I chatted about anything except what had just transpired. "I want to take Crystal to see a movie. I think it will be the best thing for her right now."

"I like that idea, Eric."

Crystal remained silent all the way home in the backseat.

When we walked in the house, I found a note from Stacy on the kitchen table. "Mom, I went to Patty's, Love Stacy."

My weary shoulders eased slightly, after the earlier tense meeting with Jerry and the Grand Jury. I trudged down the hall and entered my bedroom. I was overly numb from the events of the day. Eric and Crystal scurried to the front door. She yelled out, "Bye, Mom!"

Alone at last! Silence settled around me like a gentle sea breeze. It feels soothing. I slowly relaxed on my soft bed, closed my eyes and envisioned ocean waves softly beating against glowing white sand. Two seagulls circle in the breeze above me. Oh to be there forever! If only I could wish away all of this turmoil and agony.

My exhaustion from the past months put an unending drain on my emotions, along with my string of bad luck.

✳ ✳ ✳

Hours later, I walked to Bart's empty chest of drawers to set the alarm. Several items I had placed on the top of it were missing. That is strange. Where did those pictures of Crystal go that I left up there?

I opened the door to Bart's now empty closet. Bits of insulation and sheetrock were all over the red carpet. I peered toward the attic and saw a visible tear in the ceiling particle board that opens to the attic. Bits of insulation were on his closet shelf and rug. I knew it was possible to climb into our house from the garage, if someone entered one of the garage doors and climbed our ladder into the garage attic opening. They could easily walk across the rafters and drop down through the opening into his closet.

I hurried outside and checked the side door of the garage. It was securely locked. Next, I entered the garage and walked around our pool table and peered at the single back door. Bart had installed it years ago, after he removed the double garage doors. The closer I came to the door, the more suspicious I grew. I could see daylight shining in around the doorknob. The side of the door with the lock appeared damaged. I opened the door and discovered a cowboy boot had kicked in the door.

"That sorry son-of-a-bitch!" He must have broken into the house, while we were at his lawyer's office!"

I rushed inside, called Detective Powell and told him what I had found. "Can the police do anything about this break-in?"

"Unfortunately, they can't because..."

"I know, because our divorce isn't final yet!"

"That is correct!"

I hung up and stormed to the bedroom to check for other things Bart may have stolen. I quickly compiled a list of missing odds and ends. Nothing big. Nothing, that is, until I looked for my Magnum. It was gone. I searched everywhere for his antique gun that he gave me on that cold March morning. He stole it, too.

I drove to his apartment devoid of all logic. He had pushed me too far. The police had me completely frustrated that Bart's crimes are not crimes yet.

One more time, I turned my car into his apartment driveway and spotted his Blazer parked past the U-shaped jog. It appeared he was at Justine and Tom's apartment. I parked my car, hurried up the cement stairs and marched to their apartment door. I could see Bart and Rhonda talking with them through their sheer window curtains. I turned and walked past their window one more time.

I can't explain why I decided to walk around to Bart's apartment. I used the key I had had made weeks earlier and unlocked his door. Once I was inside his closet, I opened his brown briefcase and found the antique gun, Magnum, missing pictures of Crystal and some papers I had yet to miss. I grabbed everything and stuffed them into my now bulging purse.

It's time for me to confront the rotten bastard. I dashed out the door to his friend's apartment and pounded on their door. Bart opened it. Rhonda had already left.

I glared at him. "We need to talk!"

"So, talk."

"Alone!"

He put on his cowboy hat and followed me along the long balcony to his apartment. For once, I felt I had the upper hand. He slammed his door open, flung his hat on his bar and pivoted in anger. "Now, what the fuck do you want?"

"You broke into the house!"

"Why would I do that? It wasn't me!"

"The hell it wasn't!" I reached into my purse and pulled out the unloaded antique gun.

The moment Bart saw it, he knew I had just caught him in a major lie. *Instantly, a strange monster erupted inside of him. He streaked toward me like a screaming maniac."*

12

≈

A Sordid Trail of Lies

Bart grabbed for the gun with one hand and tore into my left arm with his other hand. *My arm felt like a shark's teeth had just ripped into my flesh. Waves of pain shot through my arm.* He snatched the gun from my hand and tried to backhand me. I ducked, grabbed his metal coasters from his bar and slammed them at his face. One of the coasters cut his lower lip. Blood spewed onto his chin and shirt. He grabbed me with both hands, shoved me backwards into a wooden chair and made that wild scream again. Then he stomped my left knee with one of his boots.

Excruciating pain tore into my knee. I felt certain my knee could be broken. *The asshole fails to realize one important matter. At that point, he is dealing with one fearless person who has no reason to live and is dangerously dead inside. At that point, pain or no pain, there is no way in hell I will give up.*

In spite of my intense pain, I raised my other foot and rammed the end of an exposed steel post on one of my high heels into his left shin bone. I raked that steel point downward and slit his pants and his shin wide open. Blood gushed everywhere. He stared at his wounded leg and then at me. "When are you going to stop fighting back?"

"You will have to kill me to stop me. Every time you hit me, I'll hit you back. I've drawn blood twice, and I will do it again!"

"You're nothing but a bitch!"

"Correct, mother fucker. You created me, and I won't back down!"

Later that night when I arrived home, Crystal and Eric saw my injuries and listened to what I went through with Bart. Crystal turned, walked to her room and wrote me a note.

"To My Mother:

I love you very much! I hope this mess soon ends because I don't think I could live through it if all my friends get dragged into it. Besides, I don't think it is worth the pain to me, and I am not very normal anymore, anyway, or at least I don't feel that way.

I can't go through with the charges. Please understand.

Love, Crystal"

The next morning Crystal put the note on our kitchen table and left with Eric.

When I woke up and walked down the hallway, I realized Stacy's room was unusually silent. He never came home from Patty's apartment last night.

I walked to the kitchen table, found Crystal's note and reread it again and again to find acceptance about her decision.

Eventually, I knew the time had come to call Detective Powell. "If Crystal can't handle the pressure, all bets are off. The charges must be dropped."

I could hear disappointment in his voice. "By the way, the Grand Jury just indicted Bart for incest ten minutes ago. I guess this means that scumbag will get off! Come by tomorrow and pick up all the photos, letters and your tape."

Next, I called my attorney. "Greg, Crystal wants to drop the charges against Bart."

"That is such bad news. I will call Jerry Kahn and work out terms for withdrawing the charges. I need to include the agreement in your divorce hearing scheduled for next week."

"Let me know when you I can sign it, and I will be there."

Later, Jerry's secretary phoned. "I set up your appointment with Jerry and Bart for eleven a.m. tomorrow. Can you make it?"

"Eleven tomorrow works for me."

My head was reeling. I sat on the den couch and dropped off to sleep. Hours later, Stacy stumbled in the front door. I sat up and went to check on him. He smelled as if he had fallen into a sewer. "Were you in a fight or something?"

"I'm sick." He ambled to the hallway bathroom and shucked his smelly clothes.

"Did someone hurt you?"

"No, Mom, let me tell you later." He drug into his room and passed out on his bed.

My spirit was downtrodden, when I met with Bart and Jerry. I cut my eyes at Bart. "I want you to sign off of any claim to the house, and you need to take over that new bill on the screened-in porch. I can't afford to pay it and feed my kids."

In an hour, we had agreed on our divorce terms that I wanted in exchange for dropping the incest charges. Jerry had his secretary draw up the agreement. We each signed it, and I dropped my copy off at Greg's office.

His secretary stopped me. "Debbie, be in court at nine a.m. next Tuesday. July first is your divorce day."

The events of the present day took a huge toll on me. I only slept a little the whole weekend. The night before our divorce hearing, all sleep escaped me. My tears didn't. *Painful emotions and memories swept through me. Buckets of tears surged down my cheeks.* The radio continually belted out more sad country songs. *My Journey of Anguish led me down an agonizing road called Memory Lane.*

Elvis Presley's song, "Fools Rush in (Where Angels Fear to Tread)," tore into the remains of my broken heart. *Happy memories of our best times swirled in my head like a speeding merry-go-round. The fun we had at our special park. Our Picture Perfect Family had merely been a Sordid Trail of Lies. The love I believed we had, evaporated in a blink. I desperately wanted it back. I hated to let go, but it had to be...*

Debbie's Picture Perfect Marriage

That was one of the darkest nights of my life. *I remember shrieks of pain ripping through my insides. I screamed at God again for answers. For some unexplainable reason, my wounded love for Bart refused to die. How can I want him back, after what he did? Even so, I still care for him.*

At six a.m., I looked in my vanity mirror and studied my red swollen eyes. I picked out Bart's favorite outfit. A beige slack set with soft pink flowers and green leaves. I wore it the day Bart unexpectedly returned to our mutual workplace eleven years ago. He had just been released from prison for burglarizing a local bank. *On this day, I want him to feel the same deep loss I feel. He needs to miss our sweet times and regret the devastation of the many lives he has left shattered in his wake.*

Our minds appeared to be on the same wave link that day. I met my attorney and sat beside him in the *Office of the Court*, when Bart entered the door. He was wearing his sleek shiny gray suit and deep turquoise blue pullover with three white buttons on the side of the neck. The same clothes he wore the first night we had a date. His hazel eyes were sunken deep into his head. He looked more like a demonic scarecrow than the Bart I once loved.

He signed all the papers and stood up to leave. "Aren't you going to court?" Greg inquired.

"I'll drop by your office later to get them." Then, he left.

The minute he was gone, my tears resurged. By the time I stood before Judge Harris, I had to wear my sunglasses. His empathetic eyes attempted to see my eyes through the dark lenses.

"Mrs. Austin, are you sure you want this divorce?"

In between my sobs and sniffles, I answered. "Yes."

An hour later, I entered my attorney's office to get my divorce papers. I was stunned to see Bart sitting in his lobby.

"Baby, I picked up your papers for you. Can I buy you breakfast one last time?"

"I suppose."

"Come with me." He gently tugged on my limp hand. We walked across the street to a fast-food restaurant and sat in a booth. My crying resumed. Bart cried with me.

"We make a fine pair!"

He squeezed my hand. "Kitten, I will always love you. Are you sure you wanted this divorce?"

My tears refused to cease. I looked at him through my dark sunglasses. "This is my third divorce, yet it is the first time I ever divorced someone I love so damn much. It hurts like hell!"

He bit his lip. "You are the best thing that ever happened to me." His voice trailed off. He began to cry again. "Are you sure we can't get back together?"

"If I give you an egg, and you smash it in your hand, can you glue it back together?"

"Not on my best day."

"That egg represents our marriage. You smashed it into a million pieces. I want you to think about something. You and Rhonda both have problems. Two sick people can never make one well."

I never touched my iced tea. Bart stood up and walked me outside with his arm around my waist.

"I guess I need to get the rest of my things from home."

"How about eight p.m. tomorrow night?

"Can I hold you one last time?" I nodded. He held me tight for the longest time without saying a word.

"Bart, why did this happen?"

"I guess I learned it from my dear old dad. That's my only explanation." His voice broke and more tears flowed.

"What do you mean, your dad?"

"I never had a girlfriend he didn't try to put the make on. And when I was only six-years-old, he would show me pictures of nude women."

My eyes fixed on Bart with disappointment. I wonder what other stories remain buried deep inside his heart that turned him into this person I no longer recognize.

"The best I can do is forgive you for what you did to Crystal and..."

Instantly, his hazel eyes turned vile. He fired brutal words of denial at me like bullets. "I never hurt Crystal! She liked what I did. We enjoyed each other. I don't need your forgiveness. I did nothing to her that she didn't encourage."

She encouraged? His claim sent me storming across the street to my car. On my way home, I felt a strong urge to turn my car around and go strangle him.

The next day, *devious demons messed with my mind.* Bart's revolting new claims about Crystal recharged my resolve to give him a special sendoff. *He just had to turn the knife in me one more time. His confession left me wondering about Crystal. Was she really a willing participant in their sexual desires for each other, instead of an abused child? That thought tore me into a thousand pieces. I didn't know who or what to believe anymore.*

Out of nowhere, a creative plan popped into my head. I drove to the nearest drugstore and found a pharmacist. "Where is your salt peter, and how much should I add per quart?"

He led me to a shelf and showed me the proper mixture on the box. "What are you going to do with this?"

"I want to fix the SOB I divorced today. He sexually abused my daughter for eleven years. Maybe he won't figure out what is causing his impotency for at least a year or more."

The pharmacist grinned. "How are you going to slip this to him?"

"His boss gave him a four-foot-tall whiskey bottle. I plan to doctor it, before he picks up his things tonight."

"It will certainly put him in his place." He chuckled.

Next, I went to the Police Station to pick up the photo album, Crystal's letters, pictures, poster, and the confession tape.

I returned home and piled his belongings on our red living room carpet. It took me a while to open the lid on the enormous whiskey bottle. I carefully measured and poured saltpeter into the tall container. Then I closed the bottle top and noticed the stuff looked as if two inches of sugar had settled in the bottom of the bottle. I shook the bottle to dissolve it. I didn't want Bart to catch on to what I had done.

Mixed emotions churned through my head, when I met Bart at the front door. Justine and Tom came along to help him. In less than an hour, they had loaded everything into their vehicles and took off. I was left alone to deal with my broken marriage, broken dreams and broken heart.

I stepped onto our front porch. The finality of the moment seemed to reach out and slap me in the face. My eleven year marriage to Bart had legally ended. The day was *July 1, 1981...*

✳ ✳ ✳

As I wandered to my bedroom, I decided to hide Bart's confession tape inside a purse in my closet. I stuffed the letters and photos into a suitcase and shoved it under my bed. I wrapped the poster in a newspaper and opened his barren closet. *My thoughts reached for any connection to--Us. God, please end this garish nightmare and return the present to--We.* I tossed the poster on his empty shelf. *The tug of yesterday feels incomprehensible. Painful memories raced toward me from all directions and thrust me deep into a Black Hole. That night I felt numb. It was as if someone had mutilated my soul and breathing should be impossible for me.*

Come morning, I accepted a hire at work. When I arrived, I fought to hide my tears and tried to cover my job. Halfway through my shift, I wore sunglasses to hide my swollen eyes and raging tears. In minutes, I found Archie sitting at his desk and sat down.

"I need to beg off and go home."

He studied me and my sunglasses. *"Gal, no man is worth all those tears. I wish you'd forget that guy. There are plenty of good men out there."*

"I know..." My voice cracked. I squeezed his hand. "Thank you."

He half-smiled at me. "Now, go home and get some rest."

I stood up, wiped away my tears and drove home.

✳ ✳ ✳

Adelle phoned me the next morning. "Debbie, I want to take you to my singles group this weekend. It is time for you to move on with your life. You will meet new men and learn how to dance."

"I don't know. It is hard to go places without Bart. It feels strange. I know you're right. Hey, I need a favor."

"What is that?"

"I gave Bart his whiskey bottle two nights ago, and I spiked it with saltpeter."

An explosion of giggles shoot through the telephone line. "Oh, Debbie, you didn't?"

"I sure did! I bet they are back together. I felt he deserved one last surprise from me. I want to drive through his apartment complex tonight. Will you drive me there?"

"Why do you want to do that?"

"I don't know. Curiosity, I guess. I need to know if they are living there or back around the corner."

"Okay. I can pick you up after work."

It was almost dark, when she arrived in her beige Oldsmobile. Five minutes later, we entered the driveway of his apartment complex. She slowly drove around the U-shaped lot. His Blazer was backed in. Her pickup was beside it.

"Damn it!"

"You knew she would be right back with him."

"Yes, but it's her kids. He can't be around children."

"Debbie, you divorced that man. There is nothing you can do to stop him now. Just accept it."

"We'll see about that." My determination to protect her children from Bart was unstoppable. Those kids need help, and there is no one else to save them, except me.

Adelle drove toward the street. She soon drove past his adjacent balcony that overlooked his apartment's grassy courtyard. Adelle yelled. "Duck!"

I rolled sideways in the front seat, almost hit my head on her dash and carefully peered at what Adelle had seen. It was Bart and Rhonda on his balcony. They were smoking and having a serious conversation. The amber building lights had cast a murky haze across the courtyard. Adelle quickly zoomed toward the street exit.

"Do you think they saw me?"

"You're safe. Honey, you can't keep this up."

"Yeah, I know. I need to move on."

✳ ✳ ✳

Two days later, Bart phoned me. "I want to talk to you. Can I take you to dinner?"

"Sure." I answered without thinking.

"How does a Greek restaurant sound?"

"Okay, I guess."

"Pick you up at eight tomorrow night?"

"That's fine."

I hung up the phone and felt torn in twenty directions for obvious reasons. My feelings for Bart make no sense to anyone, even me. *How do I protect Rhonda's kids from his evil clutches?*

Bart arrived promptly at eight with flowers in hand. He stood there dressed to the nines in his same luscious gray suit and turquoise pullover he wore on our first date. My feelings remained mangled and bruised from the events of the past four months. I struggled to hold back my tears of sorrow, as we arrived at the Greek restaurant.

He gazed into my eyes all evening like a lovesick puppy. The more he did it, the more my tears gushed. The Greek musicians finally took a break, and we finished our meal. He noticed other patrons playing songs on a Wurlitzer jukebox at the end of the dark dance floor. He stood up and joined them. I watched him choose a tune. Then, he returned, sat beside me in the booth and tenderly wrapped his arm around my shoulder.

"This next song is for you, darling."

I was in no condition for a touching gesture from him, especially when I heard the song begin to play. It was an Elvis Presley song, "Loving You."

My tears surged once more. I broke down and wept on his ever-available shoulder. He lifted my drenched chin with his thumb. "Baby, I still love you. Why not try to work things out. I will do whatever it takes."

"I need time to think about it. Crystal and Stacy might get upset. I know my family would have a fit. I just don't know."

"At least, give it some thought. I can stay at the apartment. I don't love Rhonda. She is just handy and available. I want to be home where I belong."

"We can never work things out, until you agree to get some counseling, stay at your apartment and stop seeing her. That is the only way!"

He tried to kiss me. I turned away, so he kissed my flushed cheek and drove me home. *I went to bed more alone than ever. What will tomorrow bring to my Journey of Anguish?*

During the following weeks, I spent many evenings visiting his apartment. Occasionally, I would stay overnight. We were getting along so well. Then, he made an unexpected phone call one night. "I know this may sound odd, Stacy. I want you to come over and see my apartment. I will even cook supper."

It shocked me when Stacy accepted. The inevitable seemed light years away. I began to feel better and better about Bart's sincerity. It must have been obvious because Adelle noticed my unexpectedly happy face at work one evening.

"After many months of tears and pain, what has you this happy?"

"Oh, I'm just seeing a special guy."

"Is he special new or Special Bart?"

I dropped my head. "I... I... Well, I..."

"It's that damned Bart Austin again, isn't it?"

"Yeah."

"That man violated your child. He should be dead, not seeing you! How can you love a pervert like that?"

"I know, but I... I still love him. I can't explain it. Somehow, I still do."

"He will hurt you again. The man has no conscience. Please be careful!" She walked away and left me alone to deal with her ominous warning about Bart. My common sense agreed with Adelle, but my heart refused. A tug-of-war was going on inside me. *I felt crazy inside and out.*

✳ ✳ ✳

Slowly, I closed Debbie's book. This poor woman has been through so many heartaches in her lifetime. *God, help her see through this charismatic Snake Charmer before it's too late.*

A soft young voice spoke to me in an adult like voice. "Do you have a little girl?"

I turned to find an adorable four-year-old girl with long brown curls sitting beside me on the plane. "What's your name?"

"Candice."

"Candice is a nice name. Where is your mommy?"

"In the back crying." She folded her arms like a grown-up.

"What happened to her?"

"Daddy broke her heart. When he left us, it hurt a lot."

"I had a Daddy like that. Why are you going to Paris?"

"We have court tomorrow in Paris. *Mom says that Daddy touched me in unacceptable ways, when I was three. I can't remember it.* We are going to divorce him tomorrow."

"Your mom is doing the right thing, Candice."

She wrinkled her nose. "I better go check on her. She is taking pills that make her sleep." She smiled and left.

I took a deep breath and continued to read Debbie Austin's tragic life story...

✳ ✳ ✳

Bart stayed on his best behavior for several weeks. He even made an appointment for us with a marriage counselor named Karla Foster. I believed this was his way of moving us to an avenue called *Forgiveness.* Even so, how can I excuse his past actions? I now live on *Hopelessness Street*, where my broken heart remains a hostage. My codependency and love addiction locked arms and begged me to scurry into Bart's eager arms. My Inner Child preferred to chase the elusive butterfly of happiness elsewhere.

Weeks passed. Bart appeared more committed to changing than ever. Our joint visits with Karla gave me a glimmer of hope. She taught me not to get sucked into Bart's sick mind games again. Also, she gave me a diagram with several games listed that I need to avoid. *Poor Little Me, Isn't it Awful, If Only I, and Yes, But; all are sympathy games.* She worked hard to help me see how Bart uses my emotions to play me.

"Debbie, the only way to win these games is to never play them. Because eventually all game players will lose, even Bart. You are entering the embryo stage of recovery."

Those fundamentals, and the ones she taught me later, formed a basis for my first healthy foundation in a recovery program. By soaking up everything I learned from her, I hoped to heal my shattered self-esteem.

Sadly, Bart did not appear to be learning much at all from Karla. I wondered how long it would take for him to snow her like he did me. Soon, she requested we meet with her again in two weeks.

That night, Bart made a request. "Babe, can I drive the old green Chevy to work today?"

"Why do you want to drive it when you have a nice Blazer?"

"I like old cars."

"Okay, I guess you can."

He kept the Chevy overnight and returned it the next day.

In no time, I tired of living in two places; Bart's apartment at night and home with Stacy and Crystal every morning and early evening. Plus, my real estate hours and working part-time at the other company had my butt dragging.

One day after school, Stacy grabbed his fishing pole, a can of worms and rode his bike to *Heritage Park*. In three hours, he returned with four nice-sized fish he had caught in the picturesque pond.

"Mom, I thought Bart wasn't seeing Rhonda anymore?"

"He's not, honey. He broke up with her."

"When I rode home just now, I saw Bart park your old Chevy in her driveway. He stepped out and walked inside."

"Are you sure?"

"Yeah. Rhonda was also in the Chevy. They went into her house together. They are still there."

"He should be at work. Are you sure it was Bart?"

"I sure am and I..."

I left Stacy in midsentence, grabbed my keys to the old Chevy and stormed out the front door. *Anger surged through every particle of my being. I ran toward that bitch's house and covered four blocks in record time.* My green Chevy was sitting in the driveway of her gray-trimmed brick house. That damned yellow spotlight that Bart had installed for her was on in the daytime. I saw no signs of life. I unlocked my car, sat behind the wheel, backed out of the driveway and sped toward home.

In minutes, I had the Chevy parked in my rear driveway. It was safely locked inside our back gate. I opened the car door for fresh air and began to remove Bart's stuff from the glove box. As I gathered his papers, *a bloodcurdling sound came out of nowhere. I turned to see Bart charge toward me. He resembled a wild banshee with bulging red eyes. I screamed in pain, after he smashed my left arm with his fist. Waves of pain ripped up my arm. Adrenaline shot through my body.* "You sorry damn bastard!"

13

≈

The World between Love and Hate

Crazy as it sounds, we had a huge fight in the front seat of that old Chevy. "What do you think you're doing, bitch?" He smashed my head against the dashboard.

I fought to protect myself and slammed my left elbow into his chest. "This is my car. I just took it back!"

"Oh no, you don't!" He squeezed my right hand and forced me to drop his papers from the glove box.

"Dammit, get off of me!" I shoved my knee into his groin with all my might. Just like in the movies, that worked out nicely. He doubled up in intense pain. It did my heart good to know he hurt.

"You're lucky I haven't already killed you. If you were a man, you'd already be dead, or at least have two broken legs by now."

"I'm not afraid of you. You destroyed my life. You are the lucky one. I could have blown your fucking head off that morning. You wouldn't have known what hit your sorry ass!"

He softened. "Baby, where does this leave us?"

"It leaves your butt out of my life. You two deserve each other. I never want to see you again!"

Tears flowed down his cheeks. He quickly backed water. "I love you, doll."

"Well, this is a damned-funny way to show it, asshole."

"Dammit, you know how much I love you." He pulled me close and kissed me. Confusion whirled in my head. One minute, he physically attacks me. The next, he kisses me as if I'm his long lost love. Before I know it, we were in our king-size bed making love again like newlyweds.

The phone rang an hour later. Crystal and Stacy weren't home. I looked at Bart. "I'm not expecting any calls. Are you?"

"Nope. I say we let it ring."

The phone rang over forty times and fell silent only to ring for forty minutes. "Do you think it could be Rhonda?"

"Probably. Let's go get a banana split."

"Great idea!" We dressed and scurried out the front door to my car. The telephone was still chiming away. We soon ordered banana splits at a Dairy Queen and chatted like young lovers from long ago.

An hour-and-a-half later, we drove back to the house. When we arrived, our neighbor from across the street, Stan Frasier, rushed to my car. He looked surprised to see me. He was almost out of breath as we got out of my car.

"Debbie, you're in one piece and so is Bart."

"Yes, we are. What's wrong?"

"The police just left here."

Bart rolled his eyes. "What did they want?"

"They received a 911 call from a lady named Rhonda and her brother, Syd. *The police said the callers insisted that you had killed Bart. For over an hour, a Swat Team swarmed your house and tried to get inside.*"

"You must be kidding!" I had to grin.

"I'm telling the truth. They even came here and talked to the police. She was hysterical and claimed you had killed Bart."

"As you can see, he is fine. We went to eat ice cream."

"I'm relieved, but the police may return. You best call them."

"Not me. Bart can handle it."

As soon as we walked into the house, he phoned the police to assure them he was still alive and in one piece. After the call, I frowned. "Now, what about Rhonda?"

"I don't know." He shrugged.

"Obviously, she won't give up. She just proved that!"

"I can handle her. Right now, I want to park my truck, so she can't find it. Otherwise, she will be back on my doorstep tonight at my apartment. Will you drive me to get my Blazer and follow me, so I can hide it while we're gone?"

"Gone where?"

"I'm not sure."

At the time, I liked his idea. We piled into my car and picked up his Blazer. He hid it across town and then sat in my passenger seat. "Take off, doll."

"What's the plan?"

"I vote we go to the horseraces." I drove home, left a note for the kids, packed a few clothes, and we left in less than an hour. Halfway there, my car had a flat tire. I stopped on the side of the road. My locking lug nut refused budge, so Bart walked a half mile to a gas station for help.

Our weekend was priceless. We won money at the races, spent quality time together in-and-out of bed, and Rhonda couldn't find Bart. The weekend ended too soon. He drove us back home. "I need to get my truck, go home and prepare for work tomorrow."

Even in the dark, I could see that something was wrong with his Blazer. "It looks as if someone broke into your truck!"

He hopped out, saw glass on the ground from his broken wing window on the driver's door and jumped inside his Blazer. He disappeared from view. In seconds, he scurried to my car window. "Someone stole my hunting rifle. I am calling the police."

"Where did you get a hunting rifle? You know you can't legally own a firearm. Before we married, you went to prison for a felony. If you call them, you'll be the one in trouble for having a rifle. Forget it. There is trouble written all over it."

"You helped me get a pardon after we married, remember?"

"Yes. I just wish you'd forget about reporting it as part of your loss to the police."

"I will be right back. I'm going to call them!"

"Please reconsider!"

He disappeared into a nearby store. Just as he returned, two officers arrived to talk with him. The lead officer approached him. "Sir, did you make a report about a truck burglary?"

"Yes, I did."

"Let's go take a look."

Bart showed them his busted window and then took the lead officer inside his Blazer. After they stepped outside, I heard Bart comment. "I am convinced that someone I work with broke into my truck."

"How can you be so sure?"

"I can tell by the missing items."

The officer looked shocked. "Other than tools, clothes, keys and legal papers, what else is missing?"

"They stole my new rifle."

"Can you describe it?"

"It has a high-powered sight, and I keep it in a brown case. My boss gave it to me in exchange for some work I did for him."

I hated to hear Bart own up to having a rifle. Gees!

"What is the ID number?"

"I can find it and call you."

"Very well, I will add it to my report. With the added value of the stolen rifle, this crime is now a felony. If we catch the thief, they will do time."

I watched the officers return to their car and leave. "Bart, I wish you would forget that rifle. It isn't worth it."

"Rhonda and Syd will pay for this."

"How can you be so sure it was them?"

"The thief smashed the window from the inside. Glass was on the ground, not inside my truck. The break is in the shape of a cowboy boot. Someone opened my truck door with a key. Rhonda has a key, so I know it was her. Damn her sorry ass!"

"How did they know where you parked it yesterday?"

"Beats me."

That question remains a mystery to this day. I drove Bart back to his apartment. He wanted to leave his truck there, until an insurance adjuster could look at it the next day. On the way to his apartment, he made an odd request. "Take me by Cotton's house."

"What for?"

"I want my rifle back."

✷ ✷ ✷

Cotton owned a home fifteen blocks from Bart's apartment. It sits in a more elite section of town. When I turned into a cul-de-sac, I parked in Cotton's driveway beside his two-story house. Bart hopped out of my car and rang the front doorbell. "No one's here!" He walked to the back door and returned. "Drive behind the house and then follow me inside."

"Not going to do that. What if they come back?"

"I just remembered, they went on a one-week deep sea fishing trip. I still have a key to his house."

"Why would Cotton give you a key to his home?"

"He was eager for me to marry Rhonda. He thought I would make a great son-in-law." I watched Bart unlock Cotton's backdoor. We entered through the kitchen. He searched every downstairs closet for his rifle.

"Come with me. I want to look upstairs." He led me by the hand up the narrow steep blue carpeted stairway. The upper rooms were much smaller than I expected. I watched him scour every bedroom closet and underneath each bed.

"Why do you think the rifle would be here?"

"Rhonda knows I could find it in her rent house because I still have a key to it."

"What is this thing you have about keys?"

He smiled. "Come on, kitten." He opened a door, leaped onto a small bed in the middle of a cozy blue room and patted it. "This used to be Rhonda's bed. I want us to make love in her bed."

For a brief moment, I hesitated, until I found something utterly satisfying about that thought. *I want to get the last laugh on Rhonda. So why not do it by sleeping with my former husband in her bed? I am greatly tempted. We made mad passionate love in her bed. I don't know which felt more exciting, the thrill of getting caught or making out in her bed with Bart.* Afterward, I smirked. Paybacks are hell, Rhonda Girl! Then I tugged on his arm. "Let's get out of here. We are pushing our luck."

"Okay, okay." We walked downstairs to the back door. "I'll be right back. Wait in the car. I forgot something."

I felt relieved, when I was out of the house and back in my Firebird. Bart soon returned to my car wearing a shit-eatin'-grin on his *El Gato face.*

"What did you do now?"

"I didn't find my rifle, so I took one of his guns."

"Put it back!"

"Aw, baby!"

"Do it right now. I mean it. I won't be party to a crime."

He slipped inside to return the gun. I had no way of knowing if he did as I asked. I could hope. Then, I drove him to his apartment. "How will you get to work tomorrow?"

"Tom will drive me. After an adjuster sees my truck, I can get it into a repair shop."

"What do you expect from her, when she returns to work?"

"Who knows? Who cares?"

I kissed him. He ambled to his apartment. Before I drove away, he tapped on my car window, so I rolled it down. "Now what?"

"It's Rhonda. She was here. I found a note on my door. Debbie, will you stay here tonight?"

"No way, she might damage my car."

"If she does, she answers to me. If you're here, I doubt she will bother me."

I agreed to stay the night. Within an hour, Rhonda banged on his door. He stepped outside to talk with her on the balcony. This time, I decided to join them.

"Look, Rhonda, you have caused enough trouble. Why not go home and take care of your kids?" My bluntness ended their visit. We walked her to her truck.

"Rhonda, Debbie and I plan to work out our problems."

Dangerous anger flashed in her eyes. She spun on her heels, bee lined to her truck and left burnt rubber in her wake.

"How will Cotton take this news?"

"I'm not sure. I'll tell him about my truck and the stolen rifle, first thing next Thursday." However, Cotton returned to work unexpectedly on Monday. Bart lasted less than an hour. Rhonda got to her daddy first. Bart told me what Cotton yelled at him.

"Get your things and never come back!"

It took a few days for Bart to find another job across town. When Rhonda found out, she paid the owner a visit and cut Bart's employment short. Her vendetta had only just begun. The next job came and went just as fast. Each time Rhonda learned where he landed a job, she had a heart-to-heart visit with the owner, and Bart became history. *Her determination to run Bart out of town helped my strategy work like a charm.*

✳ ✳ ✳

One night, I dropped by Bart's workplace. "Doll, I have something for you." He handed me a small box.

When I opened it, I was stunned. "I can't accept this!" I was staring at an enormous diamond ring. "I doubt I will ever recover from the hurt and pain of our divorce. You keep it."

I took the ring only after his repeated insistence. A few days later, Bart lost another position thanks to Rhonda, and he found another one across town. It paid less, so he was unable to cover his rent. He dropped by the house the next day. "Can I come home, until I get on my feet? I have nowhere to go."

"Not the best idea. Crystal is still living here, and I don't want any questions about property claims from you in court and..."

"I will sign a lease, anything. Doll, I am desperate."

"Why not take your ring back and sell it?"

"No, I want you to have it, and that's final. Consider the lease. I can even sleep in the garage; whatever it takes."

I knew Crystal had plans to move into an apartment with two girlfriends. "Soon, Crystal is moving in with girlfriends. If she does, you must sign a lease and expect absolutely nothing from me. I will do it to help you for a few months. That is it!"

Crystal moved two weeks later. I spoke with Stacy about Bart's request. "Sure, as long as it stays temporary."

After Bart settled into Crystal's former room, his presence made me overly nervous. It meant I had to give him a house key. *I found that thought scary as hell. Can I trust him not to steal anything?*

I hurriedly had him sign a lease and give me two month's rent. Even so, I had every reason to expect trouble from him. A week later, I washed a load of clothes and put them in the dryer. Bart tried to put his moves on me for sex right then.

In what was absolutely my last moment of weakness, he persuaded me to have sex with him. We went outside on the back patio in the hypnotic fall air and performed the act. Afterward, I mentally revisited his now infamous poem. It was like I had just brushed my teeth and felt little, if any, emotion and no enjoyment. *Touché, Mr. Snake Charmer.*

I used the supposed glow of sex to ask him a question that still gnawed at my heart. "I want to know something. Why did you need another woman, much less women, in your life?"

After a long pause came a response to top them all. *"You never shaved the top of your feet."*

His explanation left me dumbfounded. *What the hell does he mean by that remark? Who shaves the top of their feet?*

Suddenly, my dryer let out a loud squalling sound. I rushed to check on it. The dryer had totally overheated. The door was so hot, it hurt my hand. I yelled in pain. Bart dashed to the dryer with one of my oven mitts. He opened the door and removed a large pile of small hand towels from below the lint catcher. "How did all of those towels get down there?"

"Ah, you know how cheap dryers can wear out."

"It came from Sears. It wasn't cheap."

"I can take care of it." He dumped the hand towels into my trash can and left the dryer door open. "Your clothes will be okay. Just let them cool off for thirty or forty minutes."

Rhonda stayed busy doing in Bart's last job across town. Days later, he returned from work early and sat on the couch with a drained look. "Rhonda has finally succeeded in running me out of town. She just cost me another position. I think it is time for me to move to a new city and start over."

I secretly gloated. How fitting that Bart's darling mistress ran him out of town on a rail. I shook my head. "That's a real shame. Rhonda does seem driven to destroy you."

Bart packed up and prepared to leave. I returned his diamond ring, because I felt certain he stole it. As I handed it to him, I had another thought. Could this be the ring he planned to give to Rhonda when they married, or was he trying to set me up and claim I stole it from Max's house the day we went there to find his rifle?

The next day, he moved to a different city six hours away. It was a fitting end to our dysfunctional marriage.

Others had questioned my motives over the past six months, yet my *Journey through Hell* had succeeded. I kept Bart away from Rhonda's innocent little children, and let her run him out of town for me. It was also my payback to him for what he had done to Crystal,

Stacy and me. It was a tough goal to reach, yet it made the all of the insanity I had lived through well worthwhile.

✳✳✳

The time had finally arrived for me to get my life back on track. I quit selling real estate and called Archie. "Hi, I'm ready to take that full-time job you offered me. I am now the lone breadwinner for my son and me." I hoped that my path to happiness was now on my horizon.

I spent many private moments reflecting on what had happened to me and my family, after those horrific early morning hours of March 23, 1981. *In my heart, I believe, if not for the grace of God and my Angels, I could not have survived the long nightmare that began inside Bart's Blazer.*

My greatest hope now is that Crystal, Stacy, and Rhonda's children will be happy and safer in the coming years. Had I refused to listen to my Whispering Angel on that cold morning to discover Bart's disgusting trophies buried inside his Blazer, who knows what other atrocities he might have committed. In my lingering grief and despair, I pondered over what to do with so many obscene pictures of the various females who secretly slept with Bart. *The disgusting photos of Crystal clearly bothered me the worst.* I placed most of the pictures in my car, along with a pair of scissors and a big black trash bag, and drove to Heritage Park. I parked by the curb.

It took me two hours to scrutinize each photo, before I chopped each one into tiny bits. Afterwards, I tied the trash bag and dumped it into a nearby trash dumpster. *I never want them to be seen again by human eyes. Yet, I can still see them in my mind to this day.*

I hid the remaining pictures, all of the letters and poster in a secure place, in case Bart ever tried to hurt me or my children again. *One must always keep an Ace in the Hole when dealing with a lifetime criminal like Bart...*

14

≈

Water Seeks Its Own Level

That's what I've read. I enjoyed working full-time at my new job, and they liked me. Crystal sounded happy living with her two girlfriends. Stacy joined the Drama Club in high school, made new friends, and I gave him my old green Chevy to drive.

Adelle finally convinced me to visit her singles group with her. I went a few times and didn't like it. Eventually, I returned and signed up for their dance lessons. It seemed as if dancing breathed new life into me, even though I knew little about it except what I had learned from belly dancing years ago.

Somewhere in the back of my mind, I can still hear my former preacher pounding the pulpit from my teenage years. "Anyone who goes dancing will go straight to Hell." I wisely turned off that voice, enjoyed my dance lessons, made new friends and dated a few guys.

The week before Christmas, Crystal and Eric came by late one night. I could hear excitement in their voices.

"Guess what, Mom?"

"What?" Eric took Crystal's left hand. "We're engaged!" She showed me her gorgeous diamond solitaire engagement ring.

"Honey, that is wonderful!" I hugged them. "When is the big wedding day?"

"We haven't set a date yet, but soon."

"I'm ready to elope right now!" Eric grinned.

I look forward to their marriage. Everyone in our family adores Eric because he stood by Crystal, and he helped us during those highly dangerous days of the Bart ordeal.

✳ ✳ ✳

When spring arrived, Stacy spent lots of after-school time with his Drama Club friends. Usually, he would do his homework on Saturdays, yet one weekend, he headed to the front door instead.

"Where are you going?"

"I'm meeting Patty North and Angie Green from the Drama Club. We're going to hang out today."

"What about your homework?"

"I'll do it tomorrow. I want to bring Patty and Angie here one weekend to meet you." Then, Stacy rushed out the door and drove away in his old green Chevy.

✳ ✳ ✳

Mother gave me the Chevy, after I called her out on a bad day during my divorce with Bart. My anger centered on the fact that she and Harry took back my 55' Chevy, after she forced me to marry Jack. Then they kicked me out of the house with nothing but my clothes. *Twenty years later, an old wound was healed at last.*

✳ ✳ ✳

I waved goodbye to Stacy as he left to meet his girlfriends. Then I changed clothes and scurried to my car to go dancing. The traffic appeared to be light as I drove along a divided four-lane street toward the main highway. All of a sudden, the cars in front of me almost slowed to a halt. People began to honk their horns and others waved. I thought there must be a wreck ahead.

I couldn't believe my eyes when I saw Stacy sitting on a grassy, center median with Patty and Angie having a picnic and waving at cars. I honked at them. Stacy saw me and waved. *They laughed and raised their glasses in a toast. I hoped they weren't drinking anything alcoholic.*

✳ ✳ ✳

A week later, I was typing a full page ad when Lori approached me. "You have a phone call in the lunchroom."

"I do?" She nodded and walked away.

I couldn't imagine who would call me at work. "Hello?"

"Is this Ms. Debbie Austin?"

"Yes, it is"

"I'm Officer Lewis. Your son and a boy named Simon King broke into the Red Rock High School, after the guard had locked all the doors for the night."

"I can't believe my son would do that."

"This is a break-in. I'm considering taking the boys to jail."

"Please don't. Stacy's been through a lot because of my recent divorce. I'm sure there's an explanation. I'll pick them up right now, if you won't lock them up."

"I'll be right here, Ma'am."

I hung up and found Archie. "I need to leave. My son's in trouble."

"That's what moms are for, so you best get going."

Before I left, I received a second phone call in the lunchroom. "Hello?"

"Hey, it's Bart. I just arrived in town to wrap up some business. I need to pick up a few tools I left in the garage."

"I'm just now leaving work. Stacy and Simon supposedly broke into the school. Officer Lewis is waiting for me to come pick them up."

"Shucks, I'll take care of it, and when you get home, I'll buy you dinner."

When I arrived at home, Stacy had already let Bart into the house. I walked inside and said, "Where's Bart?"

"He's loading his tools from the shed into his Blazer. It made me extremely nervous to have him in my home again, without me there to monitor his actions.

Bart hurried inside the back door. "Bart, how did it go with Officer Lewis?"

"It could have been a lot worse than it was, since Officer Lewis remembered me."

"How did that happen?"

"He's the same officer who handled Crystal and Paulla, when they were caught shoplifting. I feared Stacy might be arrested if Lewis discovered Stacy's outstanding New Orleans Arrest Warrant."

"Oh, that's right."

Suddenly, Simon exited our hallway restroom and joined us in the den. Stacy turned to me. "Mom, this is Simon King. My best friend from Drama Club."

Simon approached me. He stood a head taller than Stacy, had red straggly hair, wore several earrings, makeup and mismatched clothing. He bowed in an elegant way in his *Punk Rock* clothes. "My pleasure, Madame Austin. We boys do suffer from harmless teenage curiosity."

I tried not to laugh. "Don't let it happen again."

"As heaven is my witness, it will not occur again. And now, I must take my leave. A beautiful damsel awaits my presence."

Simon scurried out the door. I chuckled. "Are all of your Drama Club friends that quirky?"

"Oh, Mom, they are all actors dying to star on Broadway."

"It certainly shows. Now, tell me how you two ended up inside a locked school building."

"We didn't do anything except walk around and look into some lockers."

"How did you get inside the school building?"

"We went to a baseball game, became bored and on the way to my car, I noticed a slightly open window. We climbed inside."

I looked at Bart. "I'm exhausted. It's late. I'm going to pass on dinner."

"I'll catch you next time. By the way, I got a job and start next week." He squeezed my hand, patted Stacy's back and took off rapidly.

My thirty-ninth birthday arrived the following week on a Saturday. I made plans to go dancing with Adelle at PWP. As I walked to my front door to leave, the doorbell rang. I opened my door to find Eric. I could tell by his face that something was terribly wrong. He dashed into the den and paced the floor.

"It's Crystal." He reached into his pocket and showed me her engagement ring, as a few tears rolled onto his cheeks.

"What in the world happened?"

"I don't know. She went out dancing with her roommates. We had a fight, and she gave me her ring back."

"Surely, this can be worked out."

"I think she met someone else at that club."

"I'm going to talk to her. She's making a huge mistake."

"You're right. I love her so much."

I hugged him. He quickly turned and left. *Has my daughter had lost her ever-loving mind to ditch such a handsome, charming guy like Eric.* I forced myself to put his news out of my mind for a while, so I could enjoy dancing that night.

The next day, I found Stacy rearranging his room. He was hanging up *Rocky Horror Picture Show* posters. I went to the kitchen and sat at my computer resting on the kitchen table. Our front screen door opened, and someone entered.

I looked around to see Crystal. "Happy Birthday, Mom." She gave me a card and placed a small potted plant on the table.

I stood up and hugged her. "Thank you, sweetheart, and what's new with you?"

She sat on the couch. "I have something exciting to tell you."

"Will I like it?"

"Maybe not, but I do. I broke up with Eric."

"Why would you do that?"

"I met someone else. His name is Oscar Reid."

"I think you may regret your decision about Eric one day. Where did you meet this guy?"

"At a country western dance hall named *Electric Cowgirl.*"

"And what attracted you to him?"

"It's the way he leans against the bar. He's a dream come true. I'm smitten by him." Her voice dripped with infatuation.

"You'll get over it. You and Eric have been together almost two years. You know what a great guy he is, and he looks just like Elvis."

"I know, Mom. I just outgrew him. You should see Oscar. He is so macho."

"Honey, this happened way too fast. You're making a big mistake! I broke up with my high school boyfriend, Roland Powers, my senior year. I've always regretted it. Don't make the same mistake I did. Take your time and think it over."

"This isn't a mistake. I'm crazy about Oscar and..."

I shook my head. "Honey, you know how much all of us adore Eric."

"It's my decision, not yours. I have to go." Crystal stormed out the front door.

Stacy wandered into the den. "Bye, Mom. I'm leaving, too."

"Where are you going?"

"Patty invited me to hang out with her and some friends."

Stacy dashed out the front door. I resumed working on my computer and tried to forget about Crystal's dumb decision. *I can only hope she comes to her senses and changes her mind about Eric, before another girl snatches him up.*

✳ ✳ ✳

The stewardess tapped me on the shoulder. "Do you prefer a sliced beef, turkey, or pastrami sandwich?"

I closed my book. "Turkey sounds about right." She handed me a sandwich.

"And to drink, I have milk, orange juice, Sprite, or Coke. There is only one Coke left."

"Give me a Coke with an Amaretto if you have it."

While she served my drinks, she opined. "Poor Crystal broke up with that adorable Eric, and we have yet to see her mysterious Oscar who can hold up a bar."

"What a foolish girl. Don't you agree that she will regret it one day?"

"I don't know. This new guy is still an unknown quantity."

"Yes, and she's following in her mother's footsteps."

The stewardess shrugged and pushed her cart down the aisle. I ate my sandwich, enjoyed my favorite drink and closed my eyes. *I fear that Debbie's children are about to disrupt her short-lived Happiness Journey.* Then I resumed reading.

✷ ✷ ✷

At work, one of the men in an adjoining department named Johnny Harper struck up a friendship with me. I found him kind, calm, easy on the eyes and married with grown kids. Even so, I liked having a friend who knew some of what I had been through with Bart and enjoyed talking with me occasionally. On my low days, Johnny would joke with me and try to cheer me up from my troubles. I would often wonder. *Why weren't any of my three husbands like Johnny? If only...*

It didn't take long for Crystal to bring Oscar to the house to meet us. He looked nothing like Eric. I glanced at him, and saw a short, stocky guy with an air of arrogance that instantly rubbed me the wrong way. She had stars in her eyes as she gushed, "Mom this is my new boyfriend, Oscar Reid."

"Ms. Austin, I want to tell you something."

"What's that?"

"I plan to marry your daughter, and I'd like your blessing."

"I'd say it is way too soon for that. You just met her."

Oscar took Crystal's hand and squeezed it. "She is all I want in a wife."

"It's best to wait and get to know each other first."

"I know all I need to know about her. She's for me."

Stacy heard us talking and came into the kitchen. He caught his first glimpse of Oscar. "Hi, I'm Stacy."

Oscar wrapped his arms around Crystal's waist from behind. "We're getting hitched real soon."

Stacy gave me his, "Is this guy for real look."

Needless to say, Oscar wasn't a big hit with either one of us. Crystal escorted him to see her old bedroom.

"Stacy, Mother and Harry will die when they hear this news."

"For sure, Mom. She's their favorite grandchild as I know. When are you going to tell them?"

"I think I'll wait until they come for their next visit. With any luck, Oscar won't last that long."

"We can only hope."

✳ ✳ ✳

Two weeks later, Mother and Harry came to the house on a Sunday afternoon. I greeted them at the door and let them sit down in the den before I broke the news.

"There's no easy way to say this. Crystal broke up with Eric several weeks ago, and she's seeing a boy named Oscar."

Momma let out a moan and rolled her eyes. "Oh no!"

Harry shook his head. "There's no one else like Eric."

"I know, and there's even more news."

Mother put her hand to her forehead. I worried that she might faint. "Please tell me this is good news."

"Oscar announced the day I met him that he plans to marry Crystal."

"We have to stop this!"

"How do we stop it, Momma? She thinks she's in love."

Mother folded her arms and began to pout. The worrisome news instantly cut their visit short. They left in a flash.

✳ ✳ ✳

A couple of weeks flew by. I noticed that Stacy was suddenly wearing a different style of clothes. I wandered in his room and sat on one of his twin beds. "Honey, I like the new look in your room. Where did your new dress style come from?"

"The Goodwill Store." He said so matter-of-factly.

"Is this a new fad for kids at school or something?"

"It's from England. It's called *Punk Rock*. Do you like it?"

"Well, it is a unique look. All teens go through a fad. I wore the first skirt above my knees in my high school. I soon became the school scandal within weeks, during my senior year."

"Did the other kids get over it?"

"Eventually they did. And many of them started to wear short skirts, too. Just wait, one day you'll be remembered as the first Punk Rocker in your school .It may take a while."

I watched him pull a black leather jacket from his closet. There were over a hundred Punk Rock pins on it. Next, he draped a black dog collar with sharp silver prongs around his neck. Then, he applied heavy eye makeup and painted a black-and-white star on one side of his face.

Stacy in Punk Rock

"I predict you will visit Principal Stinson today."

"You could be right, Mom."

"Try not to get expelled."

He quickly spiked his hair and left for school.

The next morning, he approached me in the kitchen. "You were right, Mom. Principal Stinson called me in for a talk today and asked me to tone down my look. I told him that I liked it, so he sent me home for the day to think it over."

"Were you expelled?"

"No, but he isn't going to stop me from dressing my way."

"I suggest you tone down the makeup and just wear the clothes and spiked hair for now. When the other kids begin to copy your style, Punk Rock will catch on like wildfire."

"Yeah, I could try that for a while."

It only took three weeks before Stacy was the new trendsetter at school. Many kids, especially his Drama Club friends, began to imitate his Punk Rock style.

At work, Archie pulled me aside one day. "I've been watching you. I saw how quickly you caught on to our new system. I want to put you in a course we're having next week."

"I'd like that. Thanks!"

There were twelve women, including me, in the computer class. Archie sat at the machine beside me and also took the class. When it ended talked to me privately. "No one in the course understands the new system like you. In fact, you caught on instantly. I want you to be my teacher for the other women."

"Look, I'm new here. Some people won't like me being their teacher. Are you sure about this?"

"I'm sure."

The next day, he handed me a training schedule. Archie wanted me to train two ladies at a time for a month each.

✹ ✹ ✹

Meanwhile, life at home was rarely dull moment. Crystal and Oscar showed up one Sunday. "Where's Stacy?"

"He's at Patty's apartment. What's up? You look excited."

"We joined a new church."

"What's it called?"

Oscar enlightened me. "*The Lord's Church.*"

"I never heard of it. Where do they meet?"

"It's a new denomination. We meet in the preacher's house or at a pool hall, Mom."

"A pool hall doesn't sound quite right to me."

Oscar grinned. "The preacher's going to marry us in his home."

"We are talking a year from now, aren't we?"

"Mom, July Fourth is our wedding day."

"My cousin and his band want to play for our reception."

"Crystal, have you told Mother and Harry yet?"

"No, I thought you would do that for me."

"I'd rather not."

They left as quickly as they arrived. I was heartsick over the news. I phoned Mother anyway. "Are you sitting down?"

"I am now. What's wrong?"

"Crystal and Oscar just dropped by to tell me the date for their wedding. It will be on July Fourth at their so-called preacher's house."

The conversation stopped. I knew Mother was disappointed. I'm certain the news overwhelmed her. *"Are we stuck with this Oscar guy?"*

"It sure appears that way."

Their big wedding day arrived way too soon. I finished dressing and noticed Stacy was in his room still in jeans and a t-shirt. "Aren't you going to your sister's wedding?"

"Do I have to?"

"She is our family. Come on, time to get dressed."

My disgruntled parents arrived an hour later. I swear they looked as if they were going to a funeral instead of a wedding. When we arrived at the so-called preacher's house, people were standing in the small yard. Oscar's three cousins were busy setting up their instruments outside for the reception afterward. The afternoon heat was wicked. It was the hottest day of the year.

Momma drove us there and parked her car. We exited and approached the house. Tim, Dana, and Tim's sister, Mona, arrived behind us. Crystal came to the front door in her bathrobe and hair curlers. She waved at me. "Mom, come inside to help me dress and take pictures. I followed her into a small bedroom where two of her girlfriends and Mona waited. I took photos of her while she dressed and got her hair done.

The intense heat inside the small house made it hard to breath. I caught Crystal's arm and pulled her aside. "I hope there will be some air conditioning where the wedding will take place. It's over a hundred degrees in here."

She shook her head. "No, they don't. There are big fans in the room where the wedding will happen."

"I certainly hope so." I mopped my brow.

The time for the wedding finally arrived. An escort seated me beside Tim. Momma and Harry sat behind us. Since Tim had adopted Crystal, she wanted him there. At least it wasn't Bart sitting there.

Too fast, the time arrived for the preacher to begin. I noticed his suit underarms were wet with sweat. He turned to the audience while Crystal and Oscar waited. "Is there anyone here who objects to this marriage?"

I glanced over my shoulder as Mother's hand shot up. Harry saw it and yanked her hand down. She persisted and raised it again. He yanked it down a second time. *I love my Mom!*

The so-called preacher constantly wiped his brow during the ceremony. Afterward, Stacy and Oscar cut their cake, and we hurried outside for some air. Oscar's cousins were playing music on their homemade platform.

Crystal changed clothes, and then she and Oscar stepped outside, so she could toss her bouquet. Family group photos with the bride and groom were next. The newlyweds drove away in the '70 Olds I gave to Crystal. We quickly left, and I flipped Mother's car air conditioner on to the high speed.

"What a relief, cool air at last." I sighed.

✳ ✳ ✳

A month later, I sat beside Stacy on the den couch. "What's that movie you're watching, sweetie?"

"It's called *Breaking Glass.*"

"Is something wrong?"

"No, why are you asking?"

"I don't know. You're not usually this quiet, that's all."

Later that night, I went on my first date with the local School Accountant, William Golden. I found him fun, witty and a great dancer. We spent lots of time together. It wasn't long until Mother and Harry came for a visit. William took us out for dinner. When we arrived back home, Mother made an announcement. "William, I think you're the nicest guy Debbie has ever dated."

It flattered him. "I'm just a country boy at heart."

Harry surprised me next. "Son, you are a real keeper."

I couldn't believe my ears. Mother and Harry never liked anyone that I ever dated or married in my life, and now they're actually complimenting my new boyfriend. I'm in shock!

Meanwhile at work, Johnny seemed more and more flirtatious. He boosted my bruised ego, yet I kept him on my *off limits list.* I have enough problems without getting involved with a married man.

Then Archie pulled me aside one day. *Oh no, he must be unhappy with my work?*

"I want to buy you a drink after work. I have something I want to talk over with you."

"Where are we going?"

"Meet me at the *Jockey Club* after we get off."

I entered the club and spotted Archie across the room smiling at me. I sat down, unsure of what was up.

"I think you are one talented little gal. I'd like to make you my Friday Foreman."

"You would?"

He nodded as the waitress approached. "What'll it be tonight, folks?"

"Make mine Amaretto and Coke."

Archie grinned. "Two beers in a frosted mug for me."

"Debbie, are you talking about, Sassy?"

"Of course, I am. It's obvious she doesn't like me at all."

"Let me handle her."

"I will because I don't want any trouble."

The following week was my first time as Friday Foreman and also my birthday. Sassy came to work wearing her usual scowl. She plopped into a chair by Archie's desk. I could tell from a distance, they were exchanging heated words. The next thing I knew, they walked out the side door together.

At least Archie kept his promise, when he handled Sassy's objections. He returned alone thirty minutes later and pulled me aside. "I'm going to change Sassy's hours and put her on the Sunday shift, instead. *That should fix her big mad.*"

"It works for me."

He locked up his desk and left me in charge of the small shift of Friday workers.

Lunchtime arrived, and Lori surprised me with a cake and a gift in the lunchroom. The other five ladies ate birthday cake and sang "Happy Birthday" to me. I attempted to blow out the candles, and found it impossible. Lori had used trick candles. After a big laugh, we stood up to return to work.

As we headed back to our office area, I heard a loud door slam. We turned to see someone in a colorful costume enter the side door.

It was Stacy. He strolled in dressed like *Boy George* complete with braids, a big hat, colorful costume and make-up. It left me speechless and shocked. I couldn't stop laughing as he sang a Boy George hit, "Time (The Clock of the Heart)" to me. He even did a little dance. When he finished, he handed me a flower. "Happy Birthday, Mom!" I was flattered, and it was impossible for me to regain my composure.

Needless to say, that birthday surprise from my son was a memory I'll never forget. I gave him a big hug and a kiss.

"Honey, I didn't know you could impersonate Boy George." Then I introduced him to my co-workers, and we had to return to work. Stacy left as quickly as he had arrived. *I love my son!*

✳ ✳ ✳

William and I became more serious. I began to spend weekends at his apartment. One night, I remember telling Stacy goodbye, and I walked outside toward my car. I looked up just as Oscar parked Crystal's Olds. He and Crystal stepped out and approached me. "Where are you going, Mom?"

"To William's apartment. What's up?"

Oscar wrapped his arms around Crystal's neck. "You're gonna be a grandma."

"When is this going to happen?"

"Sometime in June." Crystal beamed.

"I was hoping you'd get on your feet financially first."

"We ain't lookin' for no handout or nothin'."

"I didn't say you were."

"Mom, we'll be fine. I landed a job today at *Synnex*. My boss, Steve Simmons, is real nice and knows about the baby.

"See what I done told you," Oscar snapped. "I knew she'd gripe about the baby."

Before the conversation grew more heated, Crystal interrupted. "Come on, let's go shoot some pool." She pulled him by the hand to her car. They piled into her Olds, and he burned rubber. I slid into my car and drove to William's apartment.

When I arrived, I found him cooking supper for us. He turned around wearing an apron and kissed me. "How does a home cooked meal, dancing at *Country Time* and me for dessert sound?"

"Like music to my ears."

William made my heart sing. I found him to be kind, intelligent, and he kept me laughing. He had an animated way of talking that made the evening fun and there was a bonus; he could cook.

We arrived at *Country Time* for two hours of dancing and fun. The three-step became our specialty dance. We received many compliments. For dessert, we had out of this world sex. We made out on his carpeted bathroom floor in front of his mirrored closet. *William seems like a real gem and a keeper.*

The next week, I phoned Mother. "I have news, Momma."

"Is William going to be my next son-in-law?"

"No, but my brother isn't the only one who can make you a grandmother."

"Don't tell me. Not Crystal and Oscar!"

"Yep, I was hoping she'd wait a while. Their baby is due in June."

"Oh rats, then I guess we're stuck with Oscar."

"It sure looks that way."

I hung up just as Stacy came rushing through the front door looking as if he'd seen a ghost.

"Hi sweetheart, how was your weekend?"

He flopped on the couch and heaved a huge sigh. "Mom, you aren't going to believe what just happened to me."

"I hope it's some positive news. Your sister and Oscar came by yesterday and announced she's pregnant."

Stacy gave me the oddest look, so I sat beside him. "What's going on with you, honey?"

"Do you remember Patty?"

"Of course I do. She's the girl who climbs in your window at night to sleep with you."

"Three months ago, I was plastered and slept with her, Gwen and Amy on the same day at her apartment."

"I don't want to hear that."

"This afternoon, I went to Patty's apartment. All three of them were waiting for me to arrive."

"Okay, Stacy's here!" Patty moved beside the other girls. "We need to discuss something important with you. Why don't we go to *Chuck's Chicken* next door?"

"Great idea, I'm starved."

✴ ✴ ✴

"We went to the fast-food place, and I bought them some drinks."

"What did you think they were up to?"

"I wasn't sure, and I sure wasn't expecting what I heard."

✴ ✴ ✴

I delivered their drinks, sat down and waited for someone to speak. Amy and Gwen looked at Patty, so I looked at her.

She sputtered. "Well, Stacy, I missed my period."

"Which period was it; first, second or third period?"

"No dumbass, it wasn't my school period. It's what women have every month. It means I'm pregnant."

Amy folded her arms on the table and looked into my stunned eyes. "Sweetness, I missed my period, too."

Gwen was next. "Ditto, Stacy, you're going to be a papa, thrice."

"Oh my God, I'm fifteen-years-old. I can't have three teenage girls pregnant at the same time." I drummed my fingers on the table. "I wonder how much three abortions will cost me?"

Patty gave me her best serious look. "Stacy, we made a decision. You must choose the girl you like best and marry her. The other two girls will have their babies and allow you and your chosen lover to adopt their babies. That way the children can be raised together. It will be *Triplets by Malone*."

"This news sucks, big time."

✳ ✳ ✳

Stacy put his hand on his heart and looked at me. "Mom, I swear, my chin almost hit the floor."

"I'm getting that feeling right now."

✳ ✳ ✳

Patty nudged me extra hard. "So which one will it be?"

"Look, I like all of you. I can't choose."

"Choose, or we'll tell your Mom!"

Patty gave me a hard look. "Come on, Malone. Who is going to be your wife and the mother of your three kids?"

"Okay, if I have to choose, it's Patty! Was there ever any doubt?"

Uncontrollable laughter broke out. They never doubted that Patty would be my choice. She's my special girl. "Look girls, I guess I'll make the *Guinness World Book of Records* as the teen who knocked up three teenage girls because I decided the only honorable thing to do was to have three babies and three wives!"

✳ ✳ ✳

I held my heart in a panic. "Stacy, please tell me this is a joke!"

He leaned back on the couch, closed his eyes and continued. "We need to move in with you because Patty's Mom lives in a tiny apartment."

"You can't be serious."

"Mom, they were dead serious. They really pulled my chain."

"Gosh, you scared me half to death!" I playfully backed handed him on his arm.

✳ ✳ ✳

May first rolled around. Crystal stopped by the house. I could see she had gained lots of weight due to her pregnancy. "Mom, Steve and my co-workers gave me a baby shower at work today."

"That's nice of them. I plan to shop for baby clothes after we know if the baby is a boy or a girl."

"Look at this picture." Crystal pulled a photo from her purse. It showed her sitting in a chair at Synnex with a big bow, from one of her gifts, on top of her head.

"That's cute, honey, but how are you going to afford a babysitter while you work?"

"Steve is a great boss. He said that I can bring my baby to work, so I have no worries about a babysitter."

"Wow, that's unusually nice of him. How much longer until your delivery?"

"About two weeks."

"Do you want me there during your labor?"

"No, our preacher's wife, Patricia, is taking *Lamaze* classes with me. She's my coach."

"I hope you don't regret trying natural childbirth. Labor pains are pretty tough."

"I'll be fine. It's all about the breathing."

"Honey, I had two difficult births; one with you and also Stacy. The military refused to help mothers until their last hour with a saddle block shot or a painkiller. Trust me, it is no picnic. I'm afraid Lamaze could be a mistake."

"You're just saying that because you don't like their church."

"Those people are questionable to me."

"I like them, and that's all that matters. I need to go."

"Crystal, I hope things work out for you when the baby comes."

Two weeks later, I spent the night at William's apartment. His phone rang in the early morning hours, and he answered. "Hello?" He handed me the receiver. "Baby, it's for you."

"Mom, I'm in labor. Oscar won't get up and take me to the hospital. Please come help me!"

"That bum needs a swift kick. We'll be right there." We quickly dressed and left for Crystal's apartment. When we arrived, I knocked on their apartment door. She walked out with her packed bag. "Is Oscar awake yet?"

"No."

"I'm going to wake him up." As I barged through their doorway, Crystal's water broke. We helped her into William's car and took off for the hospital.

Patricia met us when we entered the hospital with Crystal. A nurse refused to allow me to see my daughter in her room. "Only her Lamaze coach can be in there with her, Ma'am."

I fumed to William. "I can't believe my lazy irresponsible son-in-law is asleep instead of at the hospital to see his new baby."

Quickly, I found a pay phone and called Oscar. Finally, he answered. "What?"

"Get your butt out of bed and get over here right now. No father should sleep through his child's birth!"

"I'm tired."

"Who cares? You get yourself over here right now!"

He slammed the phone in my ear. I returned to the Waiting Room and plopped beside William. "Someone looks unhappy."

"I'd like to choke that no-count SOB. He won't get up."

"You did all you could do, let it go." He patted my hand.

Thirty minutes passed. A nurse approached me. "Ms. Austin, you're daughter isn't doing very well with the pushing. She hasn't dilated enough for her baby to pass through the birth canal. She's totally exhausted. Is her husband here yet?"

"No, I can't wake him up. I'll call him again."

"Please do." The nurse scurried away.

I returned to the payphone and called Oscar until he finally answered. "I'm not asking you, I'm telling you. Get up, get dressed and get over here quick! Things aren't right. The baby is in danger." I hung up on him and returned to William.

It seemed like an eternity until the nurse returned. She led us into a hallway. I was frantic. "What's wrong?"

She frowned. *"You have a grandson. Sadly, he's blue and fighting for his life."*

Helpless twisted my heart, as I watched a different nurse through the wide nursery window. She was struggling to save my first grandchild's life. William held me. We cried together.

Suddenly, Oscar and his dad, Shorty, appeared beside us. Oscar caught my eye. "Is the baby going to live?"

"I don't know."

The four of us quietly stared through the window at the exhausted nurse. Desperation covered her strained face. It appeared hopeless for my little blue grandson. Suddenly, there was a *loud thud* beside me. Oscar's dad fainted at the sight of our tiny blue baby boy near death.

I prayed, as I watched the persistent nurse. *Relief swept over me, when my first grandchild finally released a loud cry. I knew we'd always be bonded forever.*

Crystal named him Daniel. The hospital kept him in their nursery several extra days, until he became stabilized.

Days later, I finally held little Daniel. *I can honestly say it is one of the greatest moments of my life. I smiled at my first grandson. He proved to be quite a little scrapper, just like me.*

✳ ✳ ✳

Six weeks passed when Crystal phoned me. "Mom, come get me and Daniel right away!"

"Is Daniel sick?"

"No, I'm leaving Oscar. He's been beating me up the whole time we've been married."

"Why didn't you tell me?"

"I feared what you might do after what my dad did to you."

"I'm on my way."

In short order, I picked them up, loaded their things into my car and moved them home while Oscar was at work.

I called Mother the next day. "Momma, Crystal is going to divorce Oscar. He's been beating her up. She wouldn't tell me until now because she knew I'd stop him one way or the other."

"That's the best news we've had since their wedding. Tell her we'll pay for her divorce."

I chuckled. "I sure will. She's gone to buy some diapers."

When I hung up, I peered out the bay window, spotted the creep arguing with Crystal in my front yard and rushed outside.

"Get off my property right now!"

"You can't make me. She's my wife. I want to see my son."

"You're not coming in my home. Either leave, or I call the police. We'll get a Peace Bond if we need to."

"Go ahead, bitch!"

"That does it!" I charged inside and called the police. Oscar hustled to his car and left like the coward he was for hurting Crystal.

She filed for divorce the next day. Then she made another call, hung up and grinned at me. "Steve said that I can return to work anytime. He wants to pay Daniel a dollar a day!"

"He must think a lot of you to say that."

Sixty days later, a judge signed her Divorce Decree, and we weren't rid of Oscar's meanness just yet. He moved in with his dad only blocks from my home. *Talk about shades of Tim.*

It soon became a routine for Stacy or me to babysit Daniel, while Crystal went out drinking and partying with her girlfriends.

The next thing I knew, she met a nice looking young man named Jerome Mayes. I still remember their first date. Crystal bought a new beige dress to be all dolled up for him. He surprised her when he came to our door with a beautiful yellow corsage.

Debbie's Residence

15

≈

Walk Softly on My Heart

Crystal entered my bedroom. "Mom, will you take our picture in the living room?"

"Sure I will." I grabbed my camera, followed her to the living room and took three photos of her and Jerome. They made an exceptionally attractive couple, as they left for the evening. It didn't surprise me when their dates grew more and more frequent over the next two months.

One night, I walked into the house after work and found Crystal, curled up in my grandfather's rocking chair, bawling like a baby. Her black mascara was running down her cheeks. "Honey, what's wrong?"

She blew her nose. "Jerome isn't going to see me anymore."

"What happened?"

"He's married." She whispered through her tears.

"You didn't know about this?"

"Well... I did know."

"Why in God's name would you waste your time on a married man?"

"I love him."

"No, you don't. You just divorced Oscar. You barely know this guy. This is a hard lesson that should teach you something very valuable. Avoid married men."

"I guess."

"It's time to forget that bum! He needs to go home to his wife and leave you alone."

"I don't like being alone."

"Neither do I, yet it's better than living with a liar. Honey, you're young and beautiful. There will be another guy in your life, wait and see."

Three weeks passed. I walked in from the grocery story with two sacks of groceries and stopped dead in my tracks. There sat Crystal and Jerome in my formal living room. I hurriedly put my groceries in the kitchen and returned to face them.

"What are you doing in my home? You're married. Get out of here right now and don't ever come back!"

He stood up and stammered, "Ms. Austin, I love her."

"Get out! You are not welcome here!"

Jerome left in a flash. Crystal stormed to her room and slammed her door. Daniel had been asleep in his bassinet, but the noise she made woke him up.

Things eventually returned to normal. Crystal and I spent lots of time together. She invited me to go dancing with her at *Cutters* one weekend. I drove us there and watched her and her girlfriends mount the corners of the dance floor rails and jive to the rock music. I enjoyed the entire evening, until three drinks made me dizzy and sick. I went to find Crystal.

"Sweetie, you better drive us home. I'll be in my car." I fell asleep in my backseat because my world was spinning.

Days later, Stacy stopped me on my way out the door to go dancing at a singles group. "Mom, I recently met a businessman named Bill Hanson. He's friends with Bob Hope, Liza Minnelli, Evel Knievel and many more movie stars."

"Where did you meet him?"

"At a party I went to last weekend. He wants to meet you."

"He does?"

"Yes, he made reservations for us at *L'Abandon* tomorrow night. It's an upscale French restaurant. Will you come?"

"Certainly, I'd like to meet him."

The next night, we entered the formal restaurant. I admired their two shades of blue décor with silver decorations. We followed the maître d' across the room. He led us to a table where Bill and his assistant, Dillon, were waiting. Bill rose to his feet and squeezed my hand. I quickly realized that he was quite a charmer.

"Ms. Austin, I'm most impressed with your son. He would be perfect as my Production Assistant for my upcoming movie production. There's even a small speaking part that is perfect for Stacy. What do you say about Stacy going to work for me?"

"He's still in high school. Education is the most important thing for him right now."

"I agree. I promise, his work hours will blend nicely with his school hours."

"As long as school comes first."

"Mom, I can do both."

"It has to be weekends only."

"I promise, that's all it will be." Stacy assured me.

✳ ✳ ✳

On *New Year's Eve, 1983*, a big ice storm hit our area. Stacy and Simon had planned to double date that night. Simon drove his Mom's

1975 black Cadillac Seville to pick up Stacy. When the doorbell rang, I opened the door. "Happy New Year, Simon."

He was decked out in a black coat, red tie and gray slacks. He bowed. "Enchanté, Madame Austin!"

I turned to see Stacy scurry down the hallway dressed exactly like Simon. The boys slid down our icy steps to the sidewalk and skidded to his Cadillac. Simon drove them away to pick up their New Year's Eve dates.

Crystal and I dressed in glitzy clothes and rang in *January 1, 1984*, together at *The Bell Ringer*. The whole evening with Crystal was a fun, memorable night. We laughed, giggled, flirted with the guys and brought in the New Year with champagne.

After that night, I had hopes for the coming year. Crystal seemed to have her feet on the ground. Daniel was almost two and walking everywhere. Stacy's school attendance began to suffer because he spent more of his time working for Bill.

One morning I shook his shoulder. "School starts in fifteen minutes, time to get up and get dressed."

He rolled over. "I had an argument with Bill yesterday and quit. I'll go to school tomorrow."

"Just remember, school is very important for your future."

✳ ✳ ✳

Summertime arrived. Crystal met a striking young man named Tony. According to her, "Tony has a ski boat. He wants to teach me how to water ski, and the guy is gorgeous."

I kept Daniel during her water skiing days. He and I had lots of fun together except when his *Terrible Two* behavior surfaced. He liked to follow Stacy around the house if he was home. When he wasn't there, he enjoyed rumbling through his room.

Summertime ended, and so did Crystal's involvement with Tony. Three days passed. I realized she was still in bed one morning and about to be late for work. "Are you sick today, honey?"

She began to cry. "I can't walk, Mom."

"Did you hurt yourself?"

"No, I don't know what happened. Mom, it hurts to move."

"Did you fall when you were water skiing?"

Crystal pulled her covers back and slowly tried to walk to the bathroom. It stunned me to watch her hobble along like an old woman. I helped her to the toilet. She appeared to be in terrible pain as she sat down.

"Tell me where you hurt."

"It's swollen *down there.*"

"In your pubic area?"

She raised her gown. I gasped. Her pubic area appeared to be swollen four times the average size. "I'm taking you to a hospital right now."

I woke up Stacy. "Please watch Daniel for me. I have to take Crystal to the hospital."

Next I helped her into her bathrobe, then to my car and into the ER Entrance. A nurse assisted her to a room. I sat down and watched an ER Doctor enter her room. Twenty minutes later, he sat beside me. "Ms. Austin, *Crystal has genital warts.*"

"I never heard of such a thing. Where do they come from?"

"It must be from a recent sexual partner."

"That would be Tony. How do you treat them?"

"Crystal's genital warts are *some of the worst I have ever seen.* They must be removed surgically. We'll need to keep her overnight and remove them in the morning."

I heaved a sigh. "Do whatever it takes to stop her pain."

Crystal had insurance at work, so most of her procedure was covered. I drove her home the next day. *We never spoke about it again.*

At my work, I must have appeared extremely troubled. Johnny approached me at the water fountain. "Is something wrong?"

"It's Crystal. Her behavior is out of control."

"Anytime you need to talk, I'm here."

"Thanks, Johnny. I may take you up on it."

The next week, Stacy came home and sat at the den bar. "Mom, I'm now employed at *Murphy's Restaurant* as of today."

"What about school?"

"I only work after school and weekends, plus school is almost out for the summer."

"Just don't forget that your homework takes time, too."

✳ ✳ ✳

When summertime arrived, so did a bevy of *Drama Club girls*. Either Patty, Gwen, Kacey, or Amy would enter Stacy's window to sleep with him after I fell asleep. Each morning, all traces of Stacy's nighttime visitor would be long gone. *I was clueless that my son had become such a young stud. It wasn't until I spotted a female's exposed butt exiting his window early one morning that I discovered what was happening.*

I walked into his room, just as the young girl ran off the front porch and stared at Stacy. "Who was that girl?"

"Patty."

"Was she here all night?"

"Yes."

"Has this happened before?"

"Yes."

"Is she the only one?"

"Nope."

"Remember that joke they played on you?"

Stacy nodded.

"Please don't let it become a reality. You're too young to get married or have kids. I know how tough that is, and it's even harder to be a teenager when it happens."

"I'll be careful, Mom."

Months later, I arrived home in the wee hours after dancing at the single's group. Stacy and Angie were sitting on the front steps talking in the dark. A nearby streetlight gave off some soft light across our dark yard. "What's going on tonight, kids?"

"Mom, Patty drank too much earlier tonight. I tried to grab her car keys from her. She fought me and drove away."

"Patty is one tough cookie. She'll be fine." Angie assured Stacy.

"I hope you're right." I wandered inside and went to bed.

Our doorbell went ballistic at two a.m. I hurried to open it, and found Amy and Kacey with horrified faces.

Kacey was trembling. "Patty has been in a hit-and-run accident."

"We have to wake Stacy up." Amy pleaded.

"Of course you do." Their story sounded surreal. I followed them into Stacy's room. Kacey flipped on his light and shook him. He didn't rally.

"He's a heavy sleeper like his dad."

"Stacy, wake up!" Kacey insisted.

"Go away and leave me alone!"

She became hysterical. "Stacy, this is about Patty!"

Her name rallied him. "What happened to Patty?"

"She's at *Parker Hospital!*" Amy cried out. "She's dying!"

Stacy shot half-way out of his bed and rubbed his eyes. "No, Patty can't be dying!"

"Hurry, Stacy! She may be gone before we can get there!" Kacey shouted at him.

He stood up, slipped on his clothes and shoes. "Damn it, I tried to stop her. She was so drunk that I grabbed her car keys. She fought me for them. If only I had stopped her anyway!"

Amy squeezed his arm. The girls followed Stacy out the front door to Amy's car.

I walked onto the porch and yelled at them. "Be careful!"

About six a.m., my weary son drug into the house and woke me up. He was crying. I sat up. "Did she make it?"

"No, she's gone. It was a hit-and-run on the freeway. She had a three-car wreck. One driver offered to drive her home. She refused the driver's help. As she walked across the wide freeway lanes to find a phone, a speeding car roared over the hill, hit her and kept going. The impact propelled her thirty feet through the air. Patty landed face first and slid a long way."

"A nurse broke the news to us."

"No one could discern if she was a boy or a girl, after the ambulance brought her to the ER. Unfortunately, Patty expired at four-thirty this morning."

"We drove to the freeway accident scene. I found her license plate and Volkswagen bumper along the median."

I sat up, hugged him, and we cried together. Stacy gathered some clothes and drove to Patty's apartment to be with her mother, Ann. I looked at the kitchen calendar after he left. The day was *September 15, 1984.*

✳ ✳ ✳

Days after Patty's funeral, I found Stacy resting on his bed staring at his ceiling. I entered his room and sat on the other twin bed. "How are you doing, honey?"

"A huge group of Patty's friends stayed at her apartment until her funeral. *Mom, I'd never seen a funeral before. It was barbaric. A large picture of Patty, making her skiffy wave and grin, sat on top of her coffin. I placed a pink rose beside her photo.* No one was able to console Ann or Patty's sister, Gwen. Now I... I realize that I've met a deep loneliness that will follow me for many years to come."

I reached out and held his hand.

"I don't even remember leaving the cemetery that day."

"Sweetheart, maybe it's for the best that you don't remember. I have yet to visit Granny's grave, and it's been over twelve years since she passed over. Your terrible loss will take time to heal."

16

≈

The Power of Imperfect Words

It was *Halloween, 1984*, when Crystal took a part-time job at *Murphy's* where Stacy was working. That night, I watched them create their Halloween costumes to wear to work. Before they left, I took their picture together. Crystal stopped me in the hallway. "Whose costume is the best, Mom?"

"You're both scary, so it's a tie."

"Oh Mom." Stacy teased, "You know I'm the scariest one."

"Have fun at work and drive safely. Where's Daniel?"

"Oscar wants him this weekend, so I'm going to drop him off on the way to work." She went to her room to wake Daniel up and carried him to her car. Stacy carried his diaper bag.

I watched them out the front bay window, as they left in Crystal's green Volkswagen. Not to be outdone, I dressed up like a circus clown and went to my single's group dance. They were holding a costume contest. Surprisingly, I won their "Best Costume Award."

Six weeks after Patty's funeral, I could see a significant change in Stacy. He seemed depressed and less interested in his Drama Club friends. He began to stay out late and drink more. That worried me, especially since alcoholism ran in his family.

The next day, he stopped me as I was leaving. "Mom, would you believe my sister tanked-up on the job last night?"

"I hope she doesn't get fired."

"We were serving blue beer last night because it was Halloween." He shrugged and left for school.

Before I could talk to Crystal about her drinking at work, she made an announcement. "I just quit Murphy's, and I found a new boyfriend at Synnex. So I only need to work one job now."

Soon it was almost Thanksgiving. The phone rang. "Hello."

"Mom, I just quit school. I'm going to New York with Bill and Dillon."

"Is this a joke?"

"No, school bores me. Bill wants my help on his movie. He's going to try to convince Ruth Warwick to be the star."

"What did Principal Stinson say?"

"He said that if I left, I can't come back again."

"How long will you be gone?"

"I'm not sure. I'll call you later."

"Sweetheart, I hope you won't regret this."

"I have to go, Mom. Bill is honking for me."

I hung up and phoned Mother. For the past two years, we called each other every Friday. "Momma, how are you today?"

"I'm tolerable. Your voice says something's up."

"Stacy just quit school again. He left for New York today with a producer named Bill. It worries me. Now, he'll never finish school."

"Honey, never say never because never is a long time."

"I know, Momma. You always say that."

✽ ✽ ✽

December had one unusually warm week, so Crystal and I went to frequent *Wet & Wild* several days. We poured on lots of suntan oil, found two lounge chairs near the pool and reclined to get golden tans. While we basked in the sun, she said, "Mom, I have something to tell you."

"Should I brace myself?"

"It's what I want to do. I'm moving into an apartment next week with one of the girls from work named Shirley. She has a little boy about Daniel's age. I'm so excited."

"How can you afford the rent?"

"Oh, I don't have to worry about that."

"And just why not?"

"My new boyfriend, Vince, is helping me. He's one of the top salesmen at work. He's one handsome man."

"Why is he paying your rent?"

"Because he loves me. He's also going to help me with Daniel's babysitter expenses."

"He must make lots of money."

"You should see his car. It's a black BMW."

"When do I get to meet Vince?"

"I don't know, maybe sometime after we get moved."

Within a week, Crystal and Daniel moved in with Shirley and her son. I noticed something odd. She didn't take her bed. Three weeks went by. She finally phoned me at work one day. "Hi, Mom, now that we've settled into our apartment, I want you to come over and see the place this Saturday."

"Sure, I'd like that."

On Saturday, I drove to Crystal's new abode. When I entered, she introduced me to her roommate, Shirley. She stood a head taller than Crystal and dressed as if she came from money. "I've heard a lot about you, Ms. Austin."

"All of it good, I hope."

"Yes, and Michael and I are crazy about her and Daniel." She pointed at him. "He's the man in my life." He was playing with a *Power Ranger* toy in their living room.

Crystal tugged my arm. "Mom, let me show you our room." She led me into a small bedroom. Daniel was asleep on a huge bed."

"My goodness, that's quite a bed. Where did it come from?"

"Vince bought it for us."

"He sounds like quite a guy."

Crystal beamed. "He's nothing like Oscar. He's classy, smart, kind, respects me, and he loves Daniel."

"And when do I get to meet Vince?"

Suddenly, Vince Connors, model material with dark hair and eyes, entered the room in an expensive black suit and maroon tie. "You must be Debbie."

"And you have to be Vince."

He extended his hand and abruptly stuffed it into his pocket. *It was too late. I caught a glimpse of his wedding ring.* I'm convinced my face fell. He hugged Crystal. "Catch you later, babe." Then he scurried from the room.

I glared at Crystal. "He's married!"

"He's getting a divorce."

"They all say that. This is your second married man!"

"I don't want to hear it."

"Too bad because you're going to hear it. He's paying your rent, babysitter, and obviously, he bought you this bed and..."

Crystal heaved a loud sigh of disgust.

"My daughter has no business being a kept woman. There's a name for that, and it isn't nice. It's time for you to pack up and move home with Daniel. Go tell that guy to get lost."

"No!"

"You'll call me sooner or later, after he dumps you." I wheeled on my heels and stormed out. *I fear that both of my children are teetering on the edge of disaster.*

✷ ✷ ✷

My son quit school and drove to New York with a man I barely know. My daughter is not only dating yet a second married man; she is now a kept woman. Who am I to talk? I still love a Snake Charmer who totally destroyed my life and will likely seek out more victims! God help my family.

17

≈

Down the Upward Spiral

Slowly, my *Depression Monster* returned. One weekend, I cried for three long days and nights. The Monster sucked me deeper and deeper into worthlessness. *The only thing I could hear when I cried was an evil voice chiding me. "Why are you still alive? No one cares about you! No one loves you! No one ever loved you! Why are you here? You are invisible in this world."*

I felt like a tortured soul adrift in a sea of despair. Even so, I tried my best to find something or someone to hold onto and not drown. Somehow, I managed to go to work. Johnny tried to cheer me up. "Where's that great smile of yours today?"

"I don't know. The house is empty, and both kids are off doing questionable things. Adelle just reminded me for the umpteenth time, *life isn't always fair.* I'm totally drained."

"You can always talk to me anytime, if it will help."

Johnny gave me a much needed ray of light to hold onto, and I was grateful. Later, Lori whispered in my ear. "I think Johnny's birthday is coming up. I wonder how young he'll be."

I shook my head. "Hard to tell. He looks great though."

* * *

The day was *February 20, 1985.* I decided to dust off my cake pans and bake a cake again. Later, I took a Red Velvet cake to work to surprise Johnny on his birthday. When he saw it, I thought he would be pleased. His comment hurt. "You shouldn't have done that. I don't want anyone at work to get the wrong impression."

Instantly, my face flushed. Humiliation swept through me. I rushed to the restroom before another tsunami of tears hit. The minutes inched by. My tears were out of control. Adelle became concerned about me. My ability to control my emotions had hit bottom. They began to control me, and dangerously so.

I saw myself falling further and further down a dark bottomless well of depression. I was unable to stop my nosedive. In spite of the light of day, darkness surrounded me. It was impossible for me to remain in reality. I felt myself slipping away.

At lunchtime, I sat alone at a table and stared into space. One of my so-called new friends at work approached me. Ruby Hart, an older redhead with a prissy attitude, did the most heartless thing to me, when I least needed it. She stuck her new gold ring in my face. "Look what I just bought me; a gorgeous textured lion head ring with big diamond eyes. Don't you just love it?" She gushed as she waved it in my despondent face.

At that moment, as I struggled to live, that selfish bitch shoved a damned piece of jewelry in my face knowing I was depressed. *Maybe God will forgive that selfish bitch! I studied her glowing green eyes for any sign of a heart. Finding none, I stood up and returned to work.*

I passed Adelle entering the lunchroom. I heard Ruby talk to her behind me. "Debbie will be fine. She's strong-willed! She can pull through this."

The rest of my shift remained a miserable blur. Swirling depression engulfed my tortured soul and launched me into a rapid death spiral.

After work, I struggled to see through my tears as I drove home. My depression appeared bottomless. The remaining threads of my self-esteem were being sucked down a powerful death spiral hole with me ensnared in its grasp. *It felt as if a black tornado had attached itself to the center of my chest. It was determined to suck all traces of my soul from my body.*

I don't remember arriving home. I can't do justice to any description of my pain that held me like chains of agony with each breath. I had no idea how perilously close to letting go I had become. When I entered my bedroom, a feeling unlike any I'd ever encountered in my life took over my spirit. *Suddenly, I completely lost all will to face another day; another hour, another minute. I wanted the pain to stop! I wanted out...*

I closed the door behind me and walked to Bart's side of our bed. Methodically, I sat down, opened a drawer and removed my .357 Magnum. I opened the chamber to make sure there were six hollow point bullets inside the chamber. I remember thinking; *I know this will be messy. I don't want to upset Stacy and Crystal with excessive splattered blood. Where can I sit to leave the least bloody mess for them to find?*

Straight away, I crossed a line into a strange dimension that suspended me somewhere between life and death. My lifeless eyes escorted me into a vast empty desert with no boundaries, no sound and no sign that life ever existed in that odd place. Eeriness sat beside me. A cold emptiness swept over me in search of a fresh cadaver. My decision remained absolute; I want out!

Slowly, I glanced over my right shoulder for the best bullet angle and picked up the gun with my right hand. There will be no note; no call for help and no opportunity to stop me. All I want is for this unbearable pain to end. I hurt to the core of my being. The pain remains indescribable. I must go!

Thank God, I'm leaving this hell! Then I turned the gun toward the clutching pain in my chest and... Out of the blue, my phone rang. I took one last breath and glared at it. *Why did it ring again and again? It's as if it is mocking me; timing my remaining seconds to live.* I glared at the blasted thing wishing it would disintegrate. By the 20th ring, I picked it up and placed it near my ear. I could hear Matt's voice. "Debbie, are you okay?" I hung up without a word. The persistent phone rang again for over ten minutes. Finally, I picked it up and held it near my heart. His desperate voice shot through my phone line. "Sis, can you talk to me? Did someone hurt you?"

I hung up. The phone rang incessantly for fifteen minutes. I tired of the noise and picked it up again. "Don't hang up! Honey, talk to me."

Silence echoed across my phone line for over fifteen minutes. His words failed to faze me, until a frail child-like voice came from somewhere deep inside of me. "No..." I hung up.

He called right back. Eventually, I picked up the receiver. "Sis, don't hang up. Just listen to me. I don't know what has happened to you. I'm here, and I love you very much. Don't hang up. You don't have to talk until you are ready. Will you stay on the line with me while I..."

I hung up. He called right back. I picked up the phone. "Please stay with me! Talk to me. What in God's name has happened?"

After a long pause, I fought to stop that child-like voice from whimpering a reply, but out it came... "No."

"Have you hurt someone?"

"No." It also came from that small, weak voice inside of me.

"Are you trying to hurt yourself?"

I hung up. The phone rang and rang. I picked it up in irritation. I had no plan to see or talk to anyone ever again.

"Sis, have you done something bad?"

No words could escape my lips.

"Do you want me to fly there and be with you? I'll come right now!"

"No." I heard the small voice inside me whisper.

"I'm going to stay on this phone as long as it takes. I love you! Please don't leave me!"

I hung up. He dialed my number again. I reclined on the bed with the gun in my right hand near my head. The blasted phone refused to quit ringing. My left hand put the phone near my ear. I listened to Matt talk non-stop to me for fifteen minutes. Finally, he was in tears. "Sis, promise you will be there in ten minutes, when I call back?"

My long pause must have felt like hours to him. Yet, he patiently waited for any response from me.

"Why?"

"Honey, I want you to listen to me."

"Why did you call?"

"I was watching a home movie of the time you and Mother came for a visit. You were about ten or so. Suddenly, the same feeling came over me just like the day my dad shot himself because he was dying of cancer. I ran to the phone and called you. I was certain something terrible was going on with you."

Another long pause swept through the phone line before that frail young voice inside me whispered. "It's terrible."

"Debbie, don't do this! This can't happen to me twice. Promise me you'll be there when I call back in ten minutes!"

"It's so bad!" My tiny voice stretched each word.

"Why, honey, tell me why?"

"The pain it's... it's too much."

"Can you stand it just ten more minutes? Do it for me? I'm going to call back in ten minutes. I want you to be there for me." His pleas met dead silence. "Sis, can you hear me? You mean the world to me. I love you. Will you be there in ten minutes if I hang up?"

My words were like precious pieces of time to Matt. Each one, an indication of a frail life on the other end of the line. My life literally dangled on that phone line. His only chance to change my mind hung in the balance. I tuned out each word he spoke. It took me a long time to answer him. He waited and waited and waited. Finally, he begged me. "I will *never hang up* until you promise me."

Silence followed silence. Once I decided to end my life, it was difficult to return to the other plateau; difficult to feel again; difficult to live on Earth again, or as I call it; *Hell on Earth.*

Preachers are wrong. Hell isn't after death. It lives and breathes on Earth where it dishes out misery to all inhabitants. My mind skipped further away from all desire to resume living.

"Debbie, are you there?" Matt's terrified voice shot through my receiver.

I don't remember much that he must have said to carry me back across the line between life and death. I believe it was when he talked about Divine Intervention. "God doesn't want you to die. He told me to call you. He's not ready for you to leave us yet. Obviously, He has important reasons why you must live."

Divine Intervention for me? Why does God care if I kill myself? What reason does God have to ask me to live five more seconds? I silently cross-examined *The Committee.* They are the group inside my head making decisions. *"You've had enough! It is time to let go, so do it."*

I could hear them arguing. "God doesn't care about you."

"Then, why did Matt call us?"

"It's just a fluke."

The voices chattered non-stop inside my exhausted head. I listened to them in frustration. Finally, I screamed out. *"Please help me, God!"*

Movie Debbie's Brother Watched That Day

18

≈

Divine Intervention

I came to accept that God wanted to stop me from taking my life that weekend. For several days, I revisited the events and made a conclusion. *I did experience Divine Intervention during those dark hours of my life. So, there must be a significant purpose for me to live. I made God a promise; I will not try to kill myself ever again.*

✸ ✸ ✸

A few weeks passed. One Saturday morning, I was in the kitchen fixing breakfast. I heard the front door unlock, and someone entered. I looked up to see Stacy walk in carrying his clothes. "I'm surprised to see you back from New York so soon. What happened?"

"It's a long story. I'm tired. I'll tell you later. I need some sleep." He ambled to his room, flopped on his bed and fell fast asleep.

Five days later, Crystal phoned. "Mom, can we move back home?"

"Sure, but you can't bring Vince with you."

"What does that mean?"

"It's a joke. Of course, you can come home."

In no time, things settled down. Stacy found another job waiting tables at *Junior's Café & Bar*. Crystal continued her job at Synnex. Happily, she and Vince were now history.

At work, Archie promoted me and flew me to Delaware for a week to train on a new computer system. While I was there, I went night snow skiing. It was my first time to be on snow skis. I loved it, even though I spent most of the evening riding downhill on the back of my skis.

When I returned home, I still had a gnawing lack of acceptance deep inside me about the future path of my life. I didn't want to live without a man, yet the more I dated, the more disenchanted I became. I soon turned into a serial dater; two or three dates and a guy was history. They were either too quiet, heavy drinkers, couldn't dance, were bossy or reminded me of Bart in some uncomfortable way.

One Friday night, I went dancing at my singles group. They had invited four psychics to do five minute readings for five dollars. On a whim, I decided to get one and sat down. I chose the most intellectual looking psychic. He studied the lines on my hand for a moment and studied me. *"I see extreme heartache still haunting you. There was a child involved, and you want answers. Do you have a daughter?"*

"Yes, I do."

"I see another child, a boy, who also worries you."

"That is so true."

He studied my face and seemed to see something significant about me and handed me a card. "I want you to contact this person."

"What's this for?"

"That's my mother, *Bertie Catchings*; she can help you better than I can. She sees and interprets severe issues like yours. I don't see those areas as well. Good luck." He shook my hand and wanted no money.

I stood up and returned to my seat across the floor. I stuffed her card into my purse, when a tall guy in a red James Dean jacket, named Jay Turner, asked me to dance.

For a month, I thought about that reading. I considered calling Bertie for an appointment, until things at home soon turned unpredictable. Jay and I were dating on a steady basis. We had so much fun together, until he drank and then our fun left.

And Stacy came home from *Junior's* early one night, stomped to his room and slammed the door. I was in the den watching TV. I waited and hoped he would come tell me what had happened. He never came. I went to his door, tapped on it and entered his room. I found him resting on his bed staring at the ceiling.

"Why are you home so early?"

"I don't want to talk about it."

"Is there anything I can do to help?"

"No."

I turned to leave. "Mom, my boss fired me tonight."

"There'll be other jobs." I bit my lip.

✷ ✷ ✷

Years later, Stacy finally enlightened me about what had happened on his New York trip with Bill and his job at *Junior's*.

"Bill was an exciting man to be around. He made an unsolicited call to Ruth Warrick. We drove to New York and met her on the set of *All My Children*. Ruth introduced us to most of the cast."

"That sounds quite exciting."

"She even introduced us to Langley Wallingford. I shook his hand. 'I've been a huge fan of yours since *Dark Shadows* days.' "

"Was he nice to you?"

"He said that he was flattered I remembered him."

"Next, Bill took Ruth, Dillon and me to meet Bob Hope and Ann Jillian at the *Westbury Music Fair* on Long Island. The drive back home from New York was a disaster. Friction erupted between Dillon and me. We had a fight, and I quit working for Bill. It didn't last long. Bill just now called me after I got home and rehired me."

I smiled. "I had no idea all that drama happened on your big trip."

Everything went smoothly after Stacy returned to work for Bill, until his drinking grew worse and worse. Then things came to a head with him.

Stacy later admitted. "I walked into work wearing dark sunglasses one day. Bill took one look at me. 'You're hung over today.'"

"I quit."

"I knew he was about to fire me. Today, I read a newspaper story about Bill. His company just filed for bankruptcy."

"So, time to hear your story about why you lost your job at *Junior's Bar & Grill.*"

✳ ✳ ✳

"Mom, you remember Don Long. He and I were drinking on the job. We would stash a bottle of booze from the company stock and hide it in their storeroom. The code words for us were, 'Check the storeroom ketchup bottles.' That meant it was time to get a drink from our stash."

"You're lucky the boss didn't catch you."

"Eventually, he caught me carrying out two boxes of wine glasses. He only gave me a warning. It was about that time when my drinking binges led to blackouts."

"Honey, I can't recall how many times our neighbor, John, told me that he found you passed out with your car door open. He would put you inside your car and lock the door. He knew if the police drove by and saw you, they would arrest you."

"Gosh, I had no idea John did that for me."

"Apparently, it was many times that he did it."

He continued. "My life was a blur. My drinking binges and blackouts continued to escalate."

"Well, I hope that won't happen anymore."

✳ ✳ ✳

A few weeks passed. I came home from work one afternoon and found Crystal and Steve, her Synnex boss, sitting on our front steps talking. "Hi, you two." I went inside.

Later, I approached Crystal. "Why was Steve here today?"

"He turned his company owners in to the IRS for cheating on their corporate taxes, and they fired him."

"Where is he going to work now?"

"I think his dad can help him get a job where he works."

That was the last I heard about Steve for several months.

✳ ✳ ✳

In the meantime, Jay invited me to the *Cattleman's Ball*. During dinner, I found a gorgeous solitaire diamond ring in my drink. Jay took my hand. "Will you marry me, baby?"

"No, I can't do that?"

"Darling, I'm nuts about you. What's not to love about me?"

"Please keep your ring."

"At least wear it for two weeks." He gave me a sexy wink.

"That ring won't change my mind."

He kissed my hand. "It might. You never know."

As I predicted, I later returned his ring. I adored Jay except when he was drinking, and then he became extremely hateful. Oddly, my decision about Jay prompted me to phone Bertie Catchings. I made a reading appointment for the following week.

✳ ✳ ✳

The day was *June 23, 1985.* I drove across town to Bertie's aging home and rang her doorbell. She opened her door. I smiled at a heavyset woman with long brown hair. She wore dark-rimmed glasses and a long flowing dress. When she began my reading, I took notes on a yellow writing pad.

"My dear, I see heartbreak like never before around you. I also see three children in your life."

"Heartbreak yes. Bertie, I only have two children."

"I see there was a miscarriage for you some time ago."

"Years ago, I kept complaining to my doctor about stomach pains. He decided to do a strange procedure on me in his office one day and put a hot iron up inside of me. It was archaic and extremely painful. I never heard an explanation of why he was doing it or how it would stop my pain."

"He caused you to miscarry later that night."

I found Bertie's miscarriage news hard to swallow.

"When I arrived at home later, I felt horrible and went to bed. My second husband, Tim, had gone on one of his all-night drinking binges, and I desperately needed him home to help me."

"It appears you came close to dying that night."

"I hemorrhaged, and the most of the bed was soaked in blood. Then a strange substance came out with all the blood and scared me to death. All I could do was prop my feet up on many pillows to keep them above my heart to slow the bleeding. I prayed to God for help. I so desperately needed to see a doctor, and Tim was off drunk in a bar somewhere. Honestly, I was alone, helpless and scared to death."

"The bloody substance that came out was a baby girl. You were barely two months along."

I choked up. "I never knew I was pregnant."

"That night was the beginning of the end of your marriage. You couldn't forgive Tim for not being home to help you."

"I know it changed my interest in him after that night."

Then Bertie changed the subject. "Your last husband broke your heart with other women. *Some of them were very close to you. I think one was your daughter. It looks as if they were lovers. She controlled him and thus, she controlled you."*

I nodded and bit my lip. I wanted her truth to be a lie, yet out comes more confirmation that their affair must be true.

"He fancied himself a real cowboy, in boots and hats. He was a serious chain-smoker. I see a bad temper all around him. Am I right about this man?"

"You nailed him and my daughter."

"I am being told that you must write a book."

"I don't know how to write a book."

"You are going to write your story about what happened to you and your family. The book will help you heal, and it will also speak to other women."

"I'm still in so much pain over it that I try to avoid thinking about it, if at all possible."

"Mark my words, you will write that book. *It has success written all over it."*

Soon the reading ended. Bertie gave me a hug. I drove home and fought the thought of wading through all of that devastating pain again. Reliving that horrible night and what I found in Bart's truck, on that cold March morning again, felt impossible for me to relive on paper.

✻✻✻

It was *July 20, 1985.* Crystal's birthday was nearing, so I invited her to the den for a talk.

"Sweetie, you and Daniel have been living here for two years at no cost. It's time for you to make a life for both of you."

I could see surprise written on her face. She slowly recovered. "I guess I can find a girlfriend to move in with."

"Mother and Harry helped me for a few months, after I divorced your dad, and we had to live with them. I was nineteen, found a job, moved to a big city and took you with me a few months later. You will do fine."

Two weeks after our talk, Crystal and Steve came by for a visit and sat on my den couch. *"Mom, we're getting married in September. We'd like your blessing."*

I looked at Steve in complete shock. "Aren't you married?"

"Not anymore. My divorce was finalized a few weeks ago. Truthfully, I fell in love with Crystal the first day I met her. I couldn't help myself."

"There is a significant age difference, and Crystal has Daniel."

Steve assured me. "Age won't be a factor. We love each other, and I've always wanted children."

"Then it looks like you'll be my new son-in-law." I hugged them, and they scurried out the door.

✻✻✻

While that was happening, Stacy began to frequent Punk Rock nightclubs. Once or twice a week, he'd call me around two a.m.

"Mom, I've been arrested. I'm in Detox. Will you come bail me out?"

"No, I won't. I lived through that with Tim, and I never bailed him out one time for drinking."

"What will I do?"

"I don't know."

Stacy slammed the phone in my ear only to call me back a few minutes later. "Please bail me out. This is a scary place."

"I'm sure it is, so don't get arrested again."

He slammed the phone in my ear. I tossed and turned all night. I feared that I could lose him to alcohol and drugs. The next day, he returned home in the afternoon and went into his room.

I stood at his doorway. "So you found some bail money?"

"Dad bailed me out, no thanks to you."

That afternoon, I went to a bookstore and bought a book someone at work had mentioned to me; *Tough Love*. I read it cover-to-cover in one day. It became my *Other Bible* to help me keep saying "No." When in my heart, I wanted to bail Stacy out of jail. His two a.m. phone calls became a regular occurrence. I feared he would eventually get hurt or hit someone with his car while driving drunk.

✵ ✵ ✵

On September, 20 1985, Crystal and Steve had a nice small wedding in his parent's home. There were about ten people there. I was happy for them and also for little Daniel. Afterward, I pulled Steve aside. *"You're the best thing that ever happened to Crystal. I know you'll take good care of her and Daniel."*

Steve moved them into his condo after their honeymoon. He quickly rented them an apartment. I felt pure relief. Maybe now Crystal will finally settle down, be a good wife and mother, and she can find some happiness and contentment.

After I quit dating Jay, I went to a Methodist Church singles group outing to meet different people who liked to dance. Jay arrived right after I walked into the room. In no time, I realized that he had followed me there. So I drove home early and went to bed.

At two a.m., my phone rang. It was Stacy making his usual call. "I was just arrested, Mom. Come bail me out."

"Stacy, my answer remains the same."

"I'm at the *Salvation Army De-Tox Center.*"

"You know I won't bail you out."

He slammed the phone, only to call back minutes later. "Mom, Dad says he's broke and can't bail me out."

"Good! It's about time! I'm surprised it took him so long."

"I can't stay in here. These people are crazy old drunks. I could be killed."

"You put yourself in there. You can find your own way out."

"You don't love me, or you'd help me. I hate you, bitch!"

"It's because I do love you that I can't help you."

As always, I heard that proverbial phone slam. I read a few pages in my *Tough Love* book, rolled over and fell sound asleep. About dawn, Stacy rumbled through the front door and fell into his bed. I walked to his room. "How did you get out?"

"An old man in my cell gave me the money. *He felt sorry for me.*" I turned to leave. "Can I throw a party in the garage for a few of my friends next month?"

"Don't you remember Crystal's small party six years ago? It turned into a nightmare of drunken kids everywhere. One neighbor climbed on his roof with binoculars to check out the noise, and he called the police on us."

"Please, Mom, I won't invite a big group."

"How about you redecorate Crystal's room and move into it. It's much bigger than yours. Then, we'll discuss a party."

"Okay, I can do that!"

I closed Stacy's door, so he could sleep and walked to the formal living room. For some reason, I opened a desk drawer and pulled out that yellow legal pad with my notes from Bertie Catchings. I decided to sit at the kitchen table and try to write a few pages of what could be the start of a book about Bart. Since that was what Bertie had told me to do, I wrote eight pages, read my words, got sick at my stomach and tossed the notepad back into my desk drawer. I couldn't bear to revisit such awful pain again.

Over the next few weeks, I bought paint, made curtains and let Stacy redecorate his new bedroom. His talent amazed me. The room looked *Mod* and as if a designer had done all the work.

"Honey, I love this design and the two-tone purple paint. Everything looks so great!"

The front doorbell rang. I let Crystal and Steve inside. "Come see what your brother has done to your old bedroom." They followed me to Stacy's new room.

Crystal's eyes light up. "Gee, Stacy, this looks awesome!"

Steve smiled. "One day, we're going to build a house. Maybe Stacy can give us some decorating tips."

"My son has so much talent. He never ceases to amaze me."

"So Mom, now that I finished the room, how about that party I want to throw in the garage?"

"You did say a *small pool party* with only a few friends?" I glanced at Crystal and winked. She knew what I was getting at; her *Nightmare Party* the year she graduated from high school.

✳ ✳ ✳

In *March, 1986,* super-hot temperatures happened. I came home late after a night of dancing with friends at *Cowboys* and quickly went to bed and fell asleep. Dancing was now my best outlet to relax, forget my troubles and have fun again.

About two a.m., a loud sound of thumping feet running across my roof woke me up from a deep sleep. I jumped up, raced to the patio and opened the sliding glass door. I could see two nude boys I didn't know swimming in our well lit swimming pool. *Suddenly, a nude male body flew off the garage roof into our swimming pool and startled me. I couldn't believe my eyes. It was Stacy.* I ran to get a bathrobe, returned to the den and flung the door open. There was no way to prepare for what I saw next...

The pool was now deserted, except there were two nude male bodies sexually intertwined on the patio couch inside our newly screened-in back porch. My son was one of those nude bodies.

"Stacy, get in here right now!"

He jumped up with hate-filled eyes and snarled at me in a drunken voice. "Fuck you bitch!"

I slammed the door, ran to the phone and called Tim. It took him forever to answer. "Who the hell is this?"

"Tim, I need help with Stacy right now!"

As I hung up, Stacy stumbled into the den barely holding a towel across his private parts and snapped at me, *"So what now, my righteous mother?"*

"I called Tim. He's on his way here."

"That's fuckin' great! Whatcha gonna tell the ol' boy. That his little boy's a fag?" Stacy flopped onto a chair and glared at me with droopy bloodshot eyes.

I tried to calm myself down. "If you are gay, it's time we knew it. *Your dad will never believe it.*"

"He will when I tell him."

"Don't count on it."

Tim knocked on the front door, so I let him inside. He avoided eye contact with me because he was hung-over. His wrinkled clothes and dark circled eyes worried me. He wobbled to the den, stood across the room and snarled. "What is all this about?"

"It's about Stacy. Let him tell you." Stacy glared at me as Tim sat on the couch, so I sat down.

"Now, what happened tonight, son?"

"Ask her, she's the one with the problem."

"No, I want you to tell me!"

Stacy made a hateful face. "*Everything sucks! She's a fucking bitch. You're a damned old drunk, and I'm just your sperm product.*"

Tim gave me a hateful look. "Is this it? You drug me out of bed for this?"

"Dad, the plain truth is; I'm gay! Your little boy is a fag!"

After his outburst, everyone sat motionless. Both Tim and I were trying to digest Stacy's *Coming Out* announcement.

It was a bombshell for Tim. He finally looked at Stacy with tears in his eyes. "No, you're drunk. You don't know what you're saying. No son of mine will ever be gay."

Stacy rolled his head in a mocking manner at his dad. "*It's true Dad. I'm gay, and you are my father!*"

"No!" I watched Tim put his face into his hands and cry."

Eventually, Tim left with a broken heart. Stacy stormed to his room, grabbed some clothes and took off for God knows where. I went outside, turned off the pool light and returned to bed. *Looking back, I'm certain I was in shock from the events of the past few hours.*

✷ ✷ ✷

I closed Debbie Austin's book and took a deep breath. It felt like I had just lived through her horrific nightmare with her. I closed my eyes and dozed off, only to be awakened ten minutes later by an irate drunken male passenger behind me. He and the stewardess were arguing. "You can't cut me off. I demand you sell me another fucking drink!"

"Sir, you've had plenty to drink, so I must refuse."

The man muttered a bunch of expletives and stumbled to the lavatory.

The stewardess walked past my row with a distressed look. I caught her eye. "Boys will be boys!" She gave me a thumbs-up and continued on her way. I reopened Debbie Austin's book, and I began to wonder. *Is she going to lose her son?*

Stacy's Punk Rock Art

✳ ✳ ✳

It was late the next night, when I heard Stacy's car door slam out front. He stomped in the front door. I was in the kitchen getting a soda pop from the icebox. He tossed his car keys on the den bar and stumbled down the hall to his room. He reeked of alcohol. I knew he was three-sheets-in-the-wind. When I turned around and saw his keys, I hid them in the pantry. Shortly, he returned for his keys. "Where the fuck did you put my car keys, Mother?"

"I haven't seen them."

He stormed around the end of the den bar toward me, so I stepped into the hall and went to the other side of the bar. He glared at me through the opening over the stove burners with the most evil look. Then he slammed both fists on the stovetop. "I want my keys now, bitch!"

"You're too drunk to drive." I grabbed the phone receiver. It was too late. Stacy rushed around the bar, grabbed the phone from my hand and ripped the cord out of the wall.

Suddenly, I saw flames shooting from underneath all four gas burner covers. "No, God not another house fire!"

He dashed to his new room, so I turned off the burners and grabbed mace from my purse. As I turned, he grabbed my arms. Then, he began to back me into the living room. I freed myself from his grip and aimed my mace at his face. "Either back off, or I will spray you with this!"

As if a tiny spark of sanity briefly hit him, he wheeled around, stomped down the hall to his room, slammed the door and proceeded to pulverize everything in his new bedroom. I could hear the sound of glass breaking, crashing furniture and slamming of all kinds going on in his room. He was trashing it. I knew it was a disaster in the making. I rushed next door to John's house and rang his doorbell. When I explained what had just happened, he called 911 for me and also Tim.

I waited in my front yard for the police to arrive. Soon, three police officers drove up and approached me. The lead officer was in charge. "Ms. Austin, where is your out-of-control son?"

"He's in the wreck that was once his room. Follow me."

I led them to Stacy's door. The lead officer turned to me. "Step back." When I did, they charged into his room and shut the door. A loud scuffle broke out. They were shouting; Stacy was shouting; it sounded terrible to me, so I opened the door.

"Don't hurt my boy, just stop him from trashing my home."

Stacy was like a wild unstoppable bear. The three officers kept whacking him because of his abnormal strength. Finally, they managed to handcuff Stacy and led him outside to their patrol car.

My mind whirred from the unbelievable nightmare before me. I followed them out the front door and stood on our porch. An officer shoved Stacy's head onto their patrol car hood because he was still fighting so hard against them handcuffing him.

When Stacy spotted me on the porch, he managed to raise his head up and screech at me at the top of his lungs. *"Mother, I hope you're happy! I've been arrested! I hate you! Hey, neighbors. My mother just had me arrested!"*

About that time, Tim drove up and engaged in a belligerent hand-waving shouting-match with the officers. The officers soon drove off in their patrol car with Stacy. Then Tim stormed toward me. "Just what the hell were you thinking?"

"Come inside, look at his room, and you'll understand why I called the police."

He followed me to Stacy's closed door. When I opened it, he gasped. "Dear God, it looks like a war zone." He turned and walked to his car without another word.

After all that, Tim phoned me the next day. "I just bailed Stacy out of jail. He's going to come live with me again."

Words almost failed me. "I can't believe you'd do that, after everything that's happened. *How can he ever change, if you keep on rescuing him every time he screws up?"*

"I don't want to hear that crap. I'll come by tomorrow and pick up his clothes."

I hung up the phone, and my doorbell rang. I opened the door to find Jay. "Hi, do you know how to fix a phone line that was ripped out of the wall?"

"Anything for my baby." He not only repaired the phone line, he helped me pick up the busted TV, lamps and more.

Stacy's Destroyed Room

Come morning, I phoned Mother and told her what had happened with Stacy. I knew the gay issue would be an instant turn off to her.

When I phoned Crystal with the news, she quickly changed the subject, as if ignoring the truth would make it go away. "Mom, I'm pregnant. You're going to be a grandmother again."

"Wonderful! When will our little bundle of joy arrive?"

"According to the doctor it will be in late July."

✱ ✱ ✱

Every day I wondered how things were going between Stacy and Tim. I wished Tim had left Stacy locked up for his own good. I prayed to God and asked Him to help me save my son.

※ ※ ※

Years later, Stacy and I had a long conversation about his second time to live with Tim...

※ ※ ※

Every room in Dad's house had empty beer cans scattered everywhere. He couldn't accept my gay status, especially when one of my high school friends, Alec Yates, was kicked out of his home when his parents discovered he was gay.

I knew Alec was sleeping in his car across the street from Dad's house. One night, he snuck through our unlocked back door, entered my room and fell asleep in my closet. Dad charged in my room in his BVD's, saw light coming from under my closet door and flung it open. He found Alec sitting on the floor reading a gay porn magazine. *"Stacy, get that fag out of my house right now!"*

"Two fags live here, Dad. If he goes, I go."

"You're not gay. You're my son!"

"He's my friend. If he leaves, I leave."

"Get out, now! Both of you!"

I piled my clothes into a suitcase, and Alec and I hurried out of the room. As we left, I saw Dad stumble to his room with a can of beer. I inserted a romance story from early England into his Dad's VCR. It made me laugh. Ironically, it was a story about two gays entitled *Another Country*.

We drove to Bill's apartment. He let us sleep on his floor. The next morning I used his phone to call Simon in San Francisco. "Hey, Simon, I'm flying there to see you today."

When I deplaned at the airport behind the other passengers, I easily spotted Simon. He was a head taller than anyone else. He had on his shit-eating grin atop his dark *Gothic Death Rock* attire. With his heavy black eyeliner and spiked blond hair, he appeared more like a seven-foot-tall anorexic Frankenstein.

Simon posed as I approached him. I could almost feel his deep sexy voice fill the air around me. *"What kept you so long, you whore?"*

End of Book One

✴✴✴

This is a Four Book Series